PUBLIC AND PERMANENT:
THE GOLDEN RULE
OF THE 21ST CENTURY

STRAIGHT TALK ABOUT DIGITAL SAFETY:
THE REAL CONSEQUENCES OF DIGITAL ABUSE

RICHARD GUERRY

BALBOA
PRESS
A DIVISION OF HAY HOUSE

Copyright © 2011 Richard Guerry

All rights reserved. No part of this book may be used or reproduced by any means, graphic, electronic, or mechanical, including photocopying, recording, taping or by any information storage retrieval system without the written permission of the publisher except in the case of brief quotations embodied in critical articles and reviews.

Balboa Press books may be ordered through booksellers or by contacting:

Balboa Press
A Division of Hay House
1663 Liberty Drive
Bloomington, IN 47403
www.balboapress.com
1-(877) 407-4847

Because of the dynamic nature of the Internet, any Web addresses or links contained in this book may have changed since publication and may no longer be valid. The views expressed in this work are solely those of the author and do not necessarily reflect the views of the publisher, and the publisher hereby disclaims any responsibility for them.

ISBN: 978-1-4525-0132-1 (sc)
ISBN: 978-1-4525-0134-5 (dj)
ISBN: 978-1-4525-0133-8 (e)

Library of Congress Control Number: 2010917513

The author of this book does not dispense medical advice or prescribe the use of any technique as a form of treatment for physical, emotional, or medical problems without the advice of a physician, either directly or indirectly. The intent of the author is only to offer information of a general nature to help you in your quest for emotional and spiritual well-being. In the event you use any of the information in this book for yourself, which is your constitutional right, the author and the publisher assume no responsibility for your actions.

Any people depicted in stock imagery provided by Thinkstock are models, and such images are being used for illustrative purposes only.
Certain stock imagery © Thinkstock.

Printed in the United States of America

Balboa Press rev. date: 1/11/2011

This Guide is based on the nationally acclaimed and award winning

Course to Digital Consciousness™ Live Event

FOREWORD

Conventional wisdom tells us that life is a game of chance. Interesting concept. After all, that's how I met Richard Guerry. It was a matter of chance.

I'm the editor of several publications – and in a very broad sense, my focus is child safety. It's a very depressing job at times, but it's important.

So a couple of years ago, on a not-so-very-special day, I went to work. On this particularly ordinary day, I followed my regular routine: I boarded a not-so-very-memorable flight and traveled to yet another national conference where I'd learn the latest things children and teens were doing that put them in dangerous situations.

In the very first session, I learned that kids were engaged in a risky new trend: Sexting. The sleeping writer inside me woke up. Great word, I thought. Not "sending sexy pictures and sexy text messages" but "sexting!"

It took all of two seconds for me to decide that this brand new and very alarming trend – sexting – was going to be my next feature.

When the day's sessions finally wrapped up, I decided to forgo a drink at the hotel bar and a dip in its tempting pool. Because I had work to do.

I spent that evening locating every sexting expert I could find. Through a series of e-mail exchanges with a handful of people, I narrowed my list of experts down to a half-dozen: Richard was one of them.

As luck would have it – or perhaps just by chance, Richard and I are from the same little corner of the world. So, I made plans to meet with him when I returned from the conference.

During our meeting, a big red flag popped up: Richard told me that sexting wasn't really the issue – it was more than that. This was not what I wanted to hear. I wanted to talk about sexting – the focus of my next article.

However, experience had taught me that I could let people chat about whatever they wanted – and then I'd be able to jump in and guide the conversation. This was my plan … so I let Richard talk. An hour and a half later, he stopped talking.

I remember this as clearly as I would if it had happened yesterday: I looked at Richard for a moment, shook my head and said, "I don't even know what to say."

I was dumbfounded. I'd never felt so "wrong" about something in my life. I went into our meeting with a clear agenda – finding out about this brand new sexting problem. Furthermore, I had every intention of guiding the conversation back to the subject when I knew Richard wanted to talk about more than just sexting.

But in that hour-and-a-half span, I learned a lot – and it changed my mind. It changed my perspective, and it changed the way I use technology. What I learned in that meeting, you will read about in this book.

The truth is the issue isn't just sexting, sexcasting or sextortion. Those are buzzwords that sensationalize the consequences when people misuse technology.

And the good news is: Richard's book reminds us that we don't have to reinvent the wheel to get this problem – irresponsible use of technology – under control.

While I'm often skeptical of solutions that sound too easy, I've also learned that our perceptions often make life harder and more complicated than it actually is. Being aware of this is the first step toward finding the solutions we need.

So today, perhaps you picked this book up on a whim – by chance.

I am confident that after you read this book, when you put it down, you'll be aware that life is more than just a game of chance.

It's also the result of our collective choices accumulated over time. And this book will remind you – and help you remind your children – that making responsible decisions is the key to staying out of trouble in all aspects of life – even in our virtual lives.

I believe in Richard's "Course to Digital Consciousness" so much that I've publicly endorsed the program; I've encouraged my own readers to adopt the philosophy; and I've recommended his "Live Event" to everyone who asks for my opinion on the best way to teach children and teens about online safety.

- Carol Warner,
School Safety Publications Editor

ABOUT THE AUTHOR

Richard Guerry is the founder of the non-profit organization, The Institute for Responsible Online and Cell-Phone Communication (IROC2). Throughout the 1990's and the turn of the 21st century, Richard served as an interactive marketing executive who achieved the position of media director by the age of twenty-eight. In his tenure, Richard strived to prevent children from viewing objectionable content online. As a result of this constant initiative, he encountered some of the darkest areas of the Internet and discovered countless individuals who were unknowingly being manipulated and scammed. What's worse, many users' content was also being stolen and exploited. He was also exposed to the myriad of ways information could be collected about a digital user through technology for marketers, and criminals. He saw firsthand how the over-sharing of information by digital citizens was creating a number of very serious, yet avoidable issues in society. As a father of two young children, and an avid user of digital technology himself, he decided to make a change and start a new revolution centered around technology – Digital Consciousness. In 2009, Richard left corporate America and applied his vast experience and knowledge of Internet safety, responsibility and citizenship to serve as the Executive Director of IROC2. He now travels across the country speaking to digital users, young and old, regarding the importance of practicing a Digital Consciousness in every aspect of life to avoid any current – or future – digital disease.

Dedicated with love and admiration to my heroic parents Patricia and Richard for whom no words could ever express my gratitude and appreciation for their love, support, guidance and strength.

ACKNOWLEDGEMENTS

Without the support, encouragement and assistance of many individuals I hold dear, my work and mission to prevent digital issues in our global community would never be possible. It is impossible to list everyone that has offered unconditional support when I decided to walk away from the corporate world to start this mission for Digital Consciousness; however, I would like to start by recognizing every member of the The Institute for Responsible Online and Cell-Phone Communication's Executive and Advisory Board members for their commitment to this cause. As for this Guide specifically? It would never have happened without the following individual's support and sacrifice and I want to express my most sincere love and gratitude to:

Richard and Patricia Guerry, who do more than tell me — they show me daily — through their heroic actions, that there is absolutely no problem that cannot be overcome. And while change is never easy, it is always possible through commitment and persistence, despite the inevitable challenges.

Bernard and Rosemarie Bricketto for their continuous love, support, generosity and assistance to me and my family, making my mission and this Guide possible.

Joshua Romano and Sandra Romano who volunteered their valuable time to review and edit this Guide. These individuals must also be recognized for their guidance and continuous support of this mission. If not for the tireless efforts of these amazing people, this Guide would never be possible.

Carol Warner for not only reviewing and editing this Guide, but for the selfless dedication to this mission. Much of what our Institute has accomplished would never have happened — and could not continue to happen — without her incredible personal and professional guidance and support.

Collin and Madeline Guerry for understanding why their father needs to travel so much, and for being a constant reminder why generations of individuals must understand how to be good digital citizens.

Jacqueline Guerry for her immeasurable support, sacrifice, love and commitment to a lofty and noble vision. There are no words that will ever justly describe what this woman means to me personally or how appreciative I am for everything that she does for our family and for IROC2. There are very few individuals that would sacrifice as much as my wife has in support of this mission to prevent digital issues in our global community

CONTENTS

PREFACE

What Is This Guide For? xix
Why Was It Written? xix
What You Need To Know Before You Get Started xx
What You Will Need xx
Thank You xxi

Intro

The Collective Passion of Secret Crowds Breaks the Cycle of Blind Insanity

Here We Go. 3

1

Marvel the Forest, Avoid the Chaos of Trees

The Case for Cause. 10
Trendy Titles 12
Informed Decision Making 14
The Digital Bystander. 15
To Be (Digital), Or Not To Be (Digital): That Is The Question 16
Taking Accountability 17
The Eyewitness Blues 19

2
The Small Town *on* Earth, Is Now the Small Town *of* Earth

The Need and Speed of Sharing 23
Face to Face-less Harassment 24
Knowledge In The Neighborhood 28
You Are In Control. 28
PRIVA-WHAT? 29
The Anon Syndrome 32
Honest Scott 34
"Passwords" or "Passing-Right-Through Words" 35
The Blame Game 40
Digital Privacy and You 41
Viruses and Spyware and Phishing, Oh My 44
Protecting Yourself and Your Data 48
Deleting & Recovering Content. 49
Your Computer's Brilliant Memory 50
Remember Me Cards 52
The Bulletin Board of the Global Village – The World Wide Web 56
You Are Historic. 58
Don't Forget The "Pocket Dial" 61

3
Our Digital Disconnect

Prevention Offline vs. Reaction Online 64
Heat Consciousness 66
Stranger (Danger) Consciousness 69
Consciousness Removal 71
A World Without Heat Consciousness. 72
A World Without Stranger (Danger) Consciousness. 75
Parental Controls Have Holes 78
Parents Just Don't Understand 79
The Rickety Bridge of Technology 80

4
Narcissistic Voyeurism Amplifies Exposure - It's All Fun and Games until Someone Uses an Eye

Narcissism Invites Voyeurism 85
The Crystal Ball Into Your Future. 86
Beware the C.E.L 87
Sexting Is Stupid 88
C.E.L's Selling You - Why Do They Do It? 91
How They Do It - Is Your Neighbor Working With A C.E.L? 93
Webcams Are a C.E.Ls Best Friend. 98
The Ripple Effect 110

5
Make Public and Permanent Work For You and Your Legacy

Public and Permanent = An Informed Decision 116
21st Century Insanity. 118
Leaving Your Digital Legacy. 118
A Digital Awakening 120
Our Digital Evolution 122

Appendix: The Workbook
Self Assessments – Guidance – Information

The Declaration of Digital Citizenship. 128
The 21st Century Flame 131
A Guide to Decision Making – Self Assessments 133
Guidance For Storing Sensitive Data 140
Opinions, Stories and Discussion Topics 142
More "Consciousness" Methodology 148
3 Frequent Ways Private Content Can Be Stolen Through Malware. . . . 153
END NOTES 155

PREFACE

What Is This Guide For?

This helpful guide was not crafted to be a technical book in as much as an informal and conversational Guide designed to communicate information and help you make smart, safe and sane decisions with your digital tools and technologies. This Guide was created to arm you with vital knowledge as if it were the missing pages of the instruction booklet for all digital tools and technologies.

Why Was It Written?

The motivation to craft this Guide stems from the overwhelming number of requests and feedback from tens of thousands of digital citizens across the U.S. between March 2009 and June 2010 seeking a literary version of the nationally acclaimed and award winning, "Course to Digital Consciousness" Live Event for which I am the primary creator and presenter.

I have had the privilege of speaking to parents, students, law enforcement and even military; in very rural areas of the United States, very wealthy areas of the United States and many places in between; and despite the differences in location and demographics of the communities I visit, the one constant message I receive is, "our town is dealing with too many digital issues."

This Guide was written to communicate to you, just as I do to those communities that I speak to, that there is absolutely no reason to "deal with" any digital issue because there is a very simple way to "prevent" any digital issue — and that is what you will understand as you read this.

What You Need To Know Before You Get Started

The events, scenarios and situations described herein are real. Names, locations, websites and imagery are censored, as I want to protect the victims you will read about. However, anyone who has attended one of The Institute for Responsible Online and Cell-Phone Communication's Live Events will confirm the legitimacy of the stories and situations provided in this Guide. One such testimonial has been provided below and you can review more at www.iroc2.org:

> "I thought your program was great and very pertinent...it's scary, but good to hear. Most of us don't think about there being this whole other side of the Internet and digital communications that you need to be wary of and consider the impact of what you are putting online or via the use of other digital communications. I liked how you provided real examples and the use of the computer to emphasize your points." –School Director from West Chester University

What You Will Need

Throughout this Guide there will be references to websites, news items and examples. You will have an opportunity to see some of the information being presented in a live Internet environment. Sometimes "seeing is believing" and where possible I will offer you real images or Internet-based exercises so you can see firsthand some of the truly unbelievable things you may discover for the first time while reading this Guide. Therefore, while not mandatory or necessary, if it is possible for you to have an Internet accessible digital device nearby, it will only enhance your experience.

Visit www.publicandpermanent.com for more information about the websites, new items and examples provided in this Guide.

Thank You

I want to thank you for taking the time to read this Guide as it clearly illustrates that you are not only dedicated to becoming an informed digital citizen, but committed to understanding how to prevent digital issues and the consequences that ensue — protecting yourself, your family and your community. Thank you for caring about our digital citizens. If we all shared the same passion, millions of current and future lives would only stand to benefit from the vast creativity, ingenuity and imagination of our evolving digital world.

THE COLLECTIVE PASSION OF SECRET CROWDS BREAKS THE CYCLE OF BLIND INSANITY

"**Insanity: doing the same thing over and over again and expecting different results.**" – Albert Einstein

"**The sane use of digital tools requires the achievement of a Digital Consciousness.**" – Yours Truly

Before we get started, I am going to ask you to do something a little unorthodox for an author who wants you to keep reading. I am going to request that you go to your computer and open up the following 3 websites:

- http://www.spokeo.com/
- http://www.peekyou.com/
- http://pipl.com/

Once you have them open, search for your name, and maybe the names of your friends, family, or even enemies. You may be astonished at what you find. You may be even more astonished to see that one of the tabs on Spokeo.com titled, "Friends" (as of September 2010) promotes their service with this text:

> Uncover personal photos, videos and secrets...
> Scan your email contacts to discover surprising facts about your friends.

You must understand that these "personal information sites" will continue to become more accurate, dig deeper and chronicle more of your digital life as we progress in this Digital Renaissance. These sites are essentially going to provide a "one-stop-shop" of information about you and your digital activity for your current and future friends, family and enemies to find. Realize that a great deal of your digital activity will be used to create your own personal digital encyclopedia entry.

Now, whether you already knew about these sites, or you are just learning about these types of websites and just had an "eye opening experience" does not matter. What matters is that you understand that there will always be some "new" trend or technology for you to discover in our rapidly evolving digital world, and your "new" discovery may not be so new for others. Therefore, to ensure you do not discover a new trend or technology the hard way — after a problem exists — we must communicate and install a preventative thought system that will help you avoid almost any digital issue or trend.

Here We Go

We cannot eliminate each new negative digital trend by reacting to it with surveys, safety tips and statistics. Reacting to digital issues is like placing a band-aid on a hemorrhaging wound. Wouldn't it be wiser to focus on preventing the injury? This Guide will illustrate how we can transform our focus on reaction to digital issues into the prevention of — current and future — digital issues.

Poor digital decision making starts in the mind – it is the "Cause" of digital mistakes. Abusing digital technology creates trends, such as sexting and cyber bullying. Those trends are the "Effects" of poor digital choices. And, as is often the case, mistakes have "Consequences" – the chain reaction of negative emotions, events and situations that follow trends.

Therefore, poor decision making – Cause – will create issues or trends – Effects – which will produce a chain reaction of negative emotions, events and situations – Consequences – as illustrated in this true story:

> A 19 year-old Wisconsin teenager was convicted of using Facebook to blackmail classmates into sex between spring 2007 and fall 2008. He was sentenced to 15 years in prison for creating a Facebook profile belonging to a nonexistent teenage girl. He used the profile to convince more than 30 of his male classmates to send in nude photos or videos of themselves. The teen then threatened to post the photos or videos of his victims — teen boys — on the Internet if they didn't engage in some sort of sexual activity with him. At least seven of his victims said they were coerced into sex acts, which were documented with a cell phone camera. (Musil, 2010) Want to read more about this? Just enter "Teen gets 15 years for Facebook blackmail" into a search engine.

As we continue to live, work and play in what I often refer to as the start of a Digital Renaissance, our global village requires a uniform social norm or "Golden Rule" to help eliminate situations like the one you just reviewed. We must establish appropriate values, beliefs, attitudes and behaviors for responsible digital decision making in our rapidly evolving digital world. This very simple but effective 21st Century "Golden Rule" is defined as: "Digital Activity Is Public and Permanent," and by understanding and employing this Golden Rule while using digital technology, you are operating with a Digital Consciousness.

Before we continue, a few things must be made extremely clear:

1) The first is that this Guide is not technical. It will not require any in depth knowledge of digital technology to understand its message.

2) The themes and information herein may seem redundant. The redundancy occurs to help you understand and develop your Digital Consciousness; to ensure you do not over-think, dilute, misinterpret or lose sight of this simple but vital thought system being introduced.

3) This Guide is not designed to focus on or react to specific issues or what I call "Effects," and it is not "the Bible" or the final authority on digital safety and citizenship. Instead, this Guide will assist you with obtaining a new and necessary mindset for using rapidly evolving digital tools and technologies. It will help you prevent issues born from ignorant or "blind" decision making when using any digital tools and technologies.

    Note: An individual that makes a decision or takes action without knowledge to evaluate all of the potential Consequences of that decision or action would be making a "blind decision" or "acting blindly." Blind decisions often lead to unexpected and sometimes tragic results. Thus, we do not have to look far beyond common sense to realize that any decision, especially when the decision involves very powerful tools and technologies, made with no information, or worse, misinformation — made blindly — would be an insane method of decision making: Blind Insanity!

4) It is important that you clearly understand what is meant by having a Digital Consciousness — having a mindset that your digital actions are public and permanent. This does not mean that every single keystroke you make or picture you take will *absolutely*

show up on the front page of a major website, an adult website, the computer of a criminal or on the news. However, having and maintaining the mindset that, "*I am prepared for the digital world and future generations to know what I am about to do with my digital device*" helps us pause and think before we act. It reminds us that it *is* possible for our digital actions to be seen by the world for generations. Therefore, it helps us evaluate risk vs. reward, it helps us to *prevent* our "private" content from becoming available to the world by never (digitally) creating it in the first place!

5) Finally, it is very important to understand that this Guide is absolutely not designed to scare or deter anyone from using digital tools and technologies. We are living, working and playing in a digital world, and to successfully communicate and succeed in each of these aspects of our lives, we must use our digital tools, but we must know how to use them responsibly, safely, and with awareness. Saying, "don't participate in sexting," "don't cyber bully," "don't talk to strangers online" is great advice, just like "don't touch a hot stove" or "don't play with matches." However, what we lack in our digital world is the communication of a preventative "consciousness" when we deliver these lessons. I will elaborate on this more throughout this Guide, however here is a brief example of this point:

We are taught from a very young age about responsible use of fire or heat before we have a chance to harm ourselves with this element. When we say "don't play with the stove" or "don't play with matches" we concurrently communicate a "Heat Consciousness." In other words, we instill knowledge that abusing fire or *any* tool that uses or creates fire (such as matches) is dangerous **because** you and your surroundings can get burned.

In a digital world however, we say things like "don't sext", "don't cyber bully", "don't do "It" (which makes some people want to do "It" more) but we neglect to accurately communicate a Digital Consciousness! The "public and permanent" thought system must be communicated *with* reactionary safety tips and advice. What we need to say is, "hey, by participating in sexting, cyber bullying (whatever the trend is), you are abusing digital technology, and abusing any digital tool is dangerous **because** what you do in a digital world is public and permanent — in just one moment you can alter your entire life and legacy."

The mass dissemination and understanding of a Digital Consciousness will ultimately construct a global digital community free from negative, life altering and tragic consequences that stem from making uninformed or *blind* decisions with digital technology. Sure, individuals and organizations will still abuse digital tools and technologies even with a Digital Consciousness, however, *with* a consciousness, they will at least *realize* they are doing it. They will have the ability to evaluate risk vs. reward. They will clearly understand the potential folly of their decision *before* they make it, which eliminates the excuse, "I didn't know" ensuring they can be (fairly) held accountable for their actions.

Think about it this way: We do not wait for a child to run towards a burning building because it might look awesome to communicate that fire can burn (Heat Consciousness). We do not wait for individuals to contract a sexually transmitted disease or become pregnant to communicate information about responsible sexual health (Sex Consciousness). We do not wait for an individual to drive recklessly harming themselves or others to provide them with the necessary information and skill sets to operate an automobile safely and responsibly (Driver Consciousness).

So why are we mass distributing rapidly evolving digital tools and technologies of incredible power to citizens across the world (including kids and criminals) without communicating a uniform social norm, a Golden Rule — a consciousness — to help citizens *prevent* mistakes that may lead to permanent and life altering consequences?

Why are we waiting for Effects like sexting, cyber bullying and sextortion to surface in media typically after a tragedy, to start trying to "deal" with them, or react to them, *after* they cause issues for so many people? Does this not seem insane when compared to how we proactively handle social and life issues offline (as illustrated in the heat, sex, and driver consciousness examples above)?

Digital technology as a whole is like water in a river — never static, constantly flowing and changing. How we use and rely on evolving (flowing) digital tools and technology will always change, as will the Consequences from our abuse. Trying to focus on all the ways our "private" content can become public and the myriad of Effects and Consequences that ensue from poor [digital] judgment is like trying to dissect, identify and review each drop of water in a river. This would be overwhelming, frustrating, unnecessary and impossible.

Throughout the remainder of this Guide, the necessity of a uniform mindset that our digital actions are public and permanent and its practice by all digital citizens will become clear. It is not only vital that you as an individual maintain this thought system when using digital tools and technologies, but it is equally as important that you become an ambassador of this information for your friends, family and peers as they can (blindly) place you at the epicenter of a very serious situation just as quickly as they can harm themselves — just ask Olympic Gold Medal winner Michael Phelps who was suspended from competition for three months by USA Swimming because of a digital photo taken by somebody else at an "event" he was attending. The photo showed the Olympic champion inhaling from a marijuana pipe. By unconditionally using digital technology responsibly, you protect yourself and your community from the negative Consequences that often accompany abuse.

Celebrities, media, and national organizations will not ultimately create the necessary shift in consciousness. You and every citizen in our global neighborhood — the "Secret Crowds" — will ultimately establish the Golden Rule of "Public and Permanent" and will break the cycle of ill-informed decision making — Blind Insanity.

Members of our global village must be independently responsible for their own actions, and it is up to each of us as individuals to change the way we think about and use digital tools and technologies — to evolve — to ultimately set an example and standard for future generations to learn from.

"Digital Consciousness" is the blue print and foundation for informed and responsible use of all current and future technology, despite application, forum, or form.

It is now time to embark on your Course to Digital Consciousness.

MARVEL THE FOREST, AVOID THE CHAOS OF TREES

Viewed as a whole, a forest radiates beauty, serenity and safety. Viewed from within, misplaced focus reaps the fabricated chaos of trees. Let me explain. Isn't it amazing how fast a forest can transform from a beautiful natural landmark to something scary and dangerous if we believe we are lost? Within minutes, our good time can become unnecessarily terrifying if we think we are lost, focusing only on all of the trees that now seem to be making scary noises and closing in on us. We can become dizzy and overwhelmed looking forward, backward, and sideways in panic trying to remember how to get out; letting this unnecessary and anxiety based fear and overreaction — this fabricated chaos — prevent us from realizing that the very clear and safe man-made path through the trees and out of the forest is just a few feet ahead — and was there the entire time.

The Case for Cause

Individually, and as a global society, we must spend less time focused on the negative issues caused by poor digital judgment *(the trees)*, as we will start to feel lost, helpless and overwhelmed by the myriad of issues and stories that surface — which will lead to hasty, fear based and not always effective reactions. We do not have to look very hard to see this is already a reality in society as minors are being criminally charged for child pornography as a Consequence for sexting through the same laws designed to protect them, while officials continue to discuss and debate the fairness of the issue.

For example:

> In March 2004, a 15-year-old Pittsburgh girl was arrested for taking nude photographs of herself and posting them on the Internet. She was charged with sexual abuse of children, possession of child pornography and dissemination of child pornography. (Blue, 2009)
>
> In October 2008, a 15-year-old Newark, Ohio girl was charged with felony child pornography for sending nude photographs of herself to a classmate in a text message. (Blue, 2009)

Let's be honest: Our cell phones, our computers and our digital cameras — they don't make choices. But we do. We make decisions with our minds which lead to our actions. What requires our attention is *not* how to react to the ill effects of usage, but how to identify and resolve problems at the source; by informing the "mind" that makes our decisions. The mind is where we must focus our attention if we want to construct a community free of negative Consequences that result from blind decision making and poor [digital] judgment. The mind is where we can *prevent* current and future issues and trends; illuminating the "path" through the proverbial forest — Digital Technology — to ensure it remains safe and beautiful for everyone. To accomplish this change in thinking it is necessary that our focus immediately shifts *away* from reaction to Effects (like sexting or cyber bullying) stemming from poor digital judgment, and towards an immediate emphasis on Cause — informing the mind how to proactively employ wise digital judgment.

Without this shift in (digital) consciousness, our educational, parental, legal and social systems will foster a vicious reaction-based cycle of hysteria and insanity with each new "digital issue" and will absolutely fail to achieve any significant progress towards proactively protecting generations from their own poor judgment. We will not eliminate negative Effects and the myriad of Consequences that ensue by waiting for individuals and organizations to make uninformed or misinformed decisions, and then trying to catch up to the "issue" once it has left a wake of destruction in its path. This is an insane methodology. As a society, we must stop employing knee-jerk reactions to each new "trend du jour" as we learn about them through media. This error creates more government debate, legal confusion, social issues, and perpetuates a cycle of insanity — thus delaying a necessary resolution.

Society seems to be reacting to Effects like sexting on cell phones because it is a "hot topic" by:

- Creating parental controls for cell phones
- Debating sexting laws
- Putting out cell phone safety tips
- And so on

But how are these reactive measures really preparing anyone to understand how they can prevent issues with any other (current or future) digital tool? Would a sexting-based class, resource or safety guide have enlightened you about the three websites presented in the introduction to this Guide?

As websites, digital tools, digital gaming and virtual reality worlds evolve, we will be inundated with even more digital device or technology-related safety tips as more inevitable issues arise from the (sometimes blind) abuse of these innovations. These new "safety tips" will illustrate another example of reaction — an example of preparing society to deal with issues only after a new trend or problem is discovered. This is insane.

Trendy Titles

In 2010 society and media were heavily focused on buzz words such as sexting and cyber bullying, but did you know that these issues have been prevalent in our society for many years prior to 2010? If I asked you to define sexting in 2007 would you have been able to? Sexting was rampant as far back as (and prior to) 2007, but unfortunately it took a number of high profile incidents and victims to make this Effect "new" in 2009 and 2010.

Society's knee jerk reaction to sexting and cyber bullying based tragedy is frightening to me. We are trying to disseminate information in schools, homes, and government about these trends, but only *after* these trends reached main stream media, and only *after* they have left a path of destruction in the lives of so many, for so long. These destructive trends flew under the radar for close to a decade until a handful of tragic Consequences resulting from this digital abuse became large enough to be "news worthy," bringing these old trends to (new) light in society.

Think about this for a moment. Aren't we seeing the typical reaction based pattern once again ring true with "Sextortion?" This "new" issue of Sextortion has been prevalent in the digital black market for many years prior to 2010, and has claimed a number of citizens' reputations. While many organizations and media outlets will begin talking about this trend more and more, understand that this is just another example of *reaction* to another buzz word, another trend!

"Sextortion" will produce new Consequences, new victims and another knee jerk reaction. Society will focus on fixing this "new" trend (that really isn't new) only *after* society becomes aware of it. Once again we will try and "fix it" by spinning our wheels on Sextortion safety tips, Sextortion surveys, Sextortion assemblies, and on and on. Why is this wasted time?

Because while we are now focusing in on Sextortion, there is another "future trend" on the horizon primed to start creating even more problems for society. Oh, and while we are shifting our attention and focus to Sextortion, we will also continue to react to sexting and cyber bullying. Gee Whiz! See how easy it is to get lost in the "forest" of Effect? See how reaction will always fail to prevent new issues?

Here is a real life example of a trend dubbed "Sextortion" that has nothing to do with sexting or cyber bullying.

> Personnel from the Criminal Investigation Department have arrested an Arab man who's believed to be the head of a network blackmailing people and extorting money from them, reports Al-Anba Daily. The Daily added that the suspect, pretending to be a female, lured victims to pose nude in chat rooms on the MSN, Yahoo messenger and Paltalk and filmed them using special built-in cameras. All the victims said they received phone calls from an unknown person asking for money followed by threats to expose these pictures through clips on the Internet website or distribute them via the Bluetooth. The source said the Criminal Investigation Department in cooperation with the Internet Service Provider (ISP) managed to identify the suspect although he used a proxy to hide his IP address. (Arab Times, 2010)

Remember, a parent or child that learns about sexting or cyber bullying will never know how to prevent Sextortion or future issues unless they concurrently receive and understand Digital Consciousness — the thought system that digital activity is public and permanent!

Sexting, cyber bullying, sextcasting, blackmail, even Sextortion and any "future trends" are nothing more than issues stemming from the abuse of digital tools and technologies. We cannot end abuse of digital tools and technologies through reaction. To cure issues stemming from digital abuse, we must fix the Cause — the mind — since this is where we decide what to do with our digital tools and technologies. If we employ a mindset that our digital activity is public and permanent, we will not be capable of making decisions under the guise of ignorance or misperception. We will all be proactively prepared and capable of preventing any "new trend."

Informed Decision Making

Sending a sexually explicit image of yourself via your cell phone with knowledge of the potential Consequences — knowing the image could become public and permanent — allows you to make an informed decision and evaluate if the potential emotional and physical suffering is worth the risks.

Do you think the girls and boys in the following story published on April 15, 2010 had a Digital Consciousness, or is their reputational and emotional suffering due to their own blind digital behavior?

> "Four 15-year-old California boys have been cited for allegedly "sexting" nude and seminude photos of eight girls ages 14-15, authorities say. The Yucaipa High School teens posted the photos to Yahoo.com's social networking message board, according to local law enforcement." (United Press International, 2010)

As this situation illustrates, we cannot correct digital mistakes after-the-fact. By waiting to react, our society has failed these boys who have been arrested. Society has also failed these girls. Consider this: arresting these 15-year-old boys will not get the girls' pictures offline and off the hard drives of strangers. Reaction to digital issues based on information obtained *after* an event or tragedy has occurred is unnecessary and insane!

Would you agree that this situation which made these kids a sexting statistic could have been prevented if the girls and boys had been taught a mindset that their digital activity was public and permanent? Even if all parties involved still took and shared those pictures after being taught that their digital activity was public and permanent, at least they would have abused their technology with knowledge!

Once reaction to an issue like "sexting" is necessary in a digital world, our energies can only be spent on minimizing the damage created from that issue, but how does this assist in the prevention of the next inevitable challenge?

Even adults are not immune to the dangers of uninformed decision making that comes from a lack of Digital Consciousness as is illustrated in the following excerpt:

> "It was a face-to-Facebook showdown at a special Board of Education meeting in Windsor Locks. The board voted to place new superintendent, David T. on administrative leave, effective immediately. It was also decided the termination process would begin."
>
> On his first day on the job as the school superintendent, David T. logged onto Facebook and posted, "If every day is like this, it'll be the best job ever." Then he recounted how he took a nap and surfed the Internet all day.
>
> No surprise here: The school board has put him on leave, and it's trying to fire him.
>
> Fighting tooth and nail to keep his job, David T. complained that his Facebook postings were "private" and shouldn't be used against him. (Buchanan, 2010)

Once again, regardless of what you want to "label" his irresponsibility as, if the mindset of this superintendent, — and millions of other individuals that post "private" messages to a global public platform called the world wide web — had a mindset that what he was writing was public and permanent, then this situation and subsequent Consequences would have been avoided.

The Digital Bystander

You do not even have to be the one using digital technology to place yourself at the center of a difficult situation. There are thousands of men and woman "flashing" their private parts at concerts, events and celebrations such as Mardi Gras in New Orleans not realizing that their one second of "exposure" for beads is being captured forever by a digital device. If you are captured digitally in an "exploitable" situation, even if only for one second, that situation is freeze framed for eternity. Where that picture may wind up (adult websites and countless hard drives) may not become clear to you until after it has happened. Think a "quick flash" of your private parts can't cause you and your family emotional or reputational suffering? Just search for a clean and non-pornographic related search term such as *mardi gras girl*" in your preferred search engine and read the search results.

> **Note:** If you do not wish to view explicit or vulgar text, you should not try this exercise. Further, it is highly recommended that you do NOT click into any specific website in the search results listings, and if you do; click at your own risk!

Here is just one more example that illustrates you do not have to be a kid to find yourself at the epicenter of a tough, embarrassing or even serious situation due to a friend's lack of digital consciousness.

> "It might have seemed funny during the party, but not so funny later when a photo surfaced of Barack Obama's chief speechwriter, Jon Favreau, groping a cardboard cutout of the administration's secretary of State, Hillary Clinton.
>
> The shot of the (then) 27-year-old writer with his hand on the (then) 60-year-old cardboard senator's breast reportedly appeared for about two hours on a Facebook page before disappearing, along with numerous other Favreau pictures, including one of him dancing with the cardboard female secretary-designate." (Malcolm, 2008)

Fortunately for Mr. Favreau, who was obviously not the person to take this picture, he was able to maintain his job despite some outcry for him to lose it. There are a lot of individuals in this world who may not have been so fortunate.

To Be (Digital), Or Not To Be (Digital): That Is The Question

We can free ourselves from suffering embarrassing or severe Consequences at the hands of our own poor digital judgment by understanding the Cause — our minds — and a confused desire for instant information with irresponsibility. We must be smart about our use of digital tools and technologies, and we must realize that too much of *anything* is never good. We should not rely on digital technology for *everything*, only what it is best suited to be used for.

Digital technology provides humans the ability to attain wants and needs conveniently and instantly, but this does not mean that digital tools should be used beyond what you would do if they did not exist!

Let's examine these thoughts through example.

Without Digital Technology *I would still*:

- Look for a weather report (on TV, the newspaper or radio)
- Get the news (on TV, the newspaper or radio)
- Call or write my friends (using my home phone or a pen and paper)
- Watch videos (on my TV or VCR)

Without Digital Technology *would I still*?

- Take a nude picture of myself (with my film camera that has to be developed by a stranger)
- Verbally harass friends or strangers (to their face)
- Research my neighbors personal information (by looking in my neighbors windows or trash)
- Tell a stranger personal information about myself (at the park, mall or other public area)
- Tell strangers when I will leave for vacation (at the park, mall or other public area)

Why are so many digital citizens willing to do things *with* digital technology such as take a nude picture, harass others, offer personal information, and so on — but not *without* it?

I will reiterate, digital technology provides humans the ability to attain wants and needs conveniently and instantly, *but this does not mean that digital tools should be used beyond what you would do if they did not exist!*

We are only at the start of this Digital Renaissance. We are still in the [digital] dark ages of what tools and technologies are to come, and the power they will provide. Since we do not have a "crystal ball" projecting future digital tools, websites or issues, we must achieve proactive and perpetual digital safety, responsibility and awareness through Digital Consciousness — through a mindset that digital actions are public and permanent.

Taking Accountability

If you burn your hand on your candle's open flame, do you blame the flame — or yourself? If you answer the flame, your anger is misplaced. *You* burned your hand through irresponsibility, thus *your* mind and its careless judgment is the *Cause*.

If you crash your car because you were speeding around a sharp turn do you blame the car — or yourself? If you answer the car, your anger is misplaced! The car crashing and the ticket you receive are consequences of your speeding. *You* were in control of the car, and you made the decision to speed around a sharp turn, thus *your* mind and its careless judgment is the Cause of the accident.

In early 2010, a Middle School Student from New Jersey asked me this question at a live event:

> *"What if I get burned by fire because my stove was defective? What if my parent's car is in an accident because the car's tire blew out? In these examples me and my parents were not doing anything wrong, but still faced negative situations because of product defects. So why can't I blame a cell phone if a picture gets out that was supposed to be private because I accidentally pocket dialed someone?"*

My response was something along the lines of:

> *"While tools like a stove or an automobile may be defective and thus cause harm without poor judgment by the end user, under this scenario of pocket dialing, the cell phone (or any digital tool) cannot take or send a picture by itself. In other words, if a picture that was supposed to be private was taken and saved to a digital device, the individual who took the picture is responsible should the picture "get out," not the phone, because only the individual could take the picture using the phone, and only the individual could save the picture to the phone.*
>
> *If the individual has a mindset that their actions would be public and permanent, maybe they never take the picture due to their understanding that it may not remain private. Further, with a digital consciousness, the individual may still take the picture, however they will take it with an ability to evaluate risk vs. reward. They will understand the potential consequences before they take the picture, and before anything negative occurs. Think of it this way, if you placed a loaded gun in your pocket, and it went off, shooting you in the leg, whose fault is it? The gun or yours? Only you could load the gun, and only you can place it in your pocket."*

The Eyewitness Blues

We watch, gossip, study and report about the tens of thousands of individuals that make irreversible and life altering "mistakes" with digital technology every day. Then we employ a reactionary response in the form of press, safety websites, legal debate, and on, and on, all ineffectively directed at "fixing" or "coping" with the issues resulting from our poor decision making. What we must do is emerge as ambassadors of Digital Consciousness to enlighten the mind; to use these negative situations as an opportunity to communicate a solution — to prevent current and future negative trends and the subsequent consequences.

Please take a moment to ponder or discuss these questions:

- How does a discussion exclusively about sexting prepare society for the next negative digital trend?

- Why are we so focused on the aftermath of misuse at a time when prevention could not be more important considering how fast technology is evolving and the permanence of the consequences?

- Why do we continue to mass distribute rapidly evolving and extremely powerful digital tools to *anyone*, regardless of criminal background and age, without concurrently offering the benefit of a guideline to ensure our "digital tools of convenience" do not become "weapons of self destruction?"

To realize true global Digital Consciousness, we need a globally known and accepted "Golden Rule" to help each of us practice and remain mindful of our individual responsibility. We must inform and prepare the public "mind" to be aware that digital actions are public and permanent, regardless of the new digital tool, website, application or even generation. Practicing and understanding this globally uniform guideline, like learning that "playing with fire can burn," will help generations of individuals be proactive to *prevent* negative digital Effects and the Consequences that ensue. This necessary and vital guideline is simple, and possessing this mindset and this behavior is to possess a Digital Consciousness.

We have a choice. We can try and change the [digital] world — or we can change how each of us behaves in a digital world. Solutions to digital issues do not exist "out there" — they exist within!

THE SMALL TOWN *ON* EARTH, IS NOW THE SMALL TOWN *OF* EARTH

"You have zero privacy anyway, so get over it" – Scott McNealy, co founder of Sun Microsystems

Not too long ago, there were places in this world where everybody in town knew your name, your address and your "business." In fact, small-town living existed for years as a foundation of society as many people reveled at the opportunity to live in communities characterized by handshakes, first name greetings and familiar faces. Despite this close knit internal structure, the geographical and technological limitations of earlier times often caused these towns to be very isolated from one another. While your mayor would stop by for weekly cups of coffee and your butcher knew your Sunday order by heart, it was also very unlikely that you would know much about the lives of people outside of your own little town. In one respect this was a drawback because you were often confined to the offerings of your own community, but on the other hand, you also had the benefit of knowing that your privacy was protected from leaking out beyond the walls of your small town.

Fast forward now to the 21st century and things have changed quite dramatically. Of course, there are still "small towns" *on* Earth — small towns with a small population. However, thanks to powerful digital tools of communication bridging our borders and generations, the traditional small towns on our planet have become extinct, as our world has been transformed into one global village – the small town *of* Earth.

A small city of 500 citizens and a metropolis of millions are no longer individual communities separated by geography; they are each equal parts of one global village. Unfortunately however, with all of the benefits that we now enjoy from this global village, we are also forced to deal with new dangers and unintended consequences.

As an example of this situation, take a look at the following scenario:

Imagine a woman in a small town of 500 people in the 1940s; a time when there was no such thing as the Internet. For this woman, the two types of personal information the other 499 people in town could know about her were:

- Information that she intentionally decided to share, such as her hobbies or her favorite radio programs.

- Information that she unintentionally shared because it was beyond her control to keep private, such as where she works, where she lives or if she was not home.

Now let's look at this same town in present day where we *do* have technology, such as the Internet. Suddenly, within seconds, billions of people can know everything that the other 499 people in town know, whether it is information that she shares intentionally (such as her favorite radio show) or unintentionally (such as her home address). All of a sudden, information that seemed OK to share with 499 of her neighbors (whether intentionally or unintentionally) might not sound as good when it's being shared with over 499 million.

The definition of "neighbor" must evolve in our mind, as we are now part of a global village, and our "neighbor" — nice or not — is no longer an individual on our street, in our complex or in our community. We must understand this! Our neighborhood is now the digital world, and our neighbors are everyone in our now global village.

Howdy Neighbor!

The Need and Speed of Sharing

What people living in small towns *on* Earth and all of us living in the small town *of* Earth have in common is that a lack of privacy largely stems from our own need to "over-share," our need to "brag" and our need to "gossip."

But why do we feel the need to "share" everything?

- Would we still feel the need to over-share information if we had a mindset that our actions are public and permanent?

- Would we over-share information if we realized that what we say today can come back to haunt us tomorrow in more ways than some of us could even imagine?

    For instance, over-sharing on social networks has led to an overabundance of evidence in divorce cases. The American Academy of Matrimonial Lawyers says eighty-one percent of its members have used or faced evidence plucked from Facebook,

MySpace, Twitter and other social networking sites, including YouTube and LinkedIn, over the last five years. (Italie, 2010)

Remember, anyone, of any age, in any size town can now share information with billions of people instantly through the World Wide Web. The faster we can share information with billions of citizens, the faster we can face negative consequences if we act irresponsibly when using a global public platform that shrinks the world into one global village.

Self Assessment Tip: Try to think in these terms when using the Internet. Forget passwords and forget privacy. When you post information to the World Wide Web about yourself or someone else, you are communicating as part of an intimate global community. You are essentially posting information on a community bulletin board in the town square. What you must consider before you post any information is that everyone in the world (with Internet access) has the ability to see and share the information you posted, and the more attention called to the information, the more attention you will receive — both positive and negative.

Once your content has been seen and shared by even just one other person — out of billions — in the global village, you can never definitively remove the information from the knowledge base of the community because anyone who has seen and saved it, can at any time, put it right back up on the bulletin board, or anywhere else in the community, whenever they want and without your permission or knowledge. Once you place your information on a bulletin board in the global village, that information is no longer yours, no longer private — and never will be again.

Face to Face-less Harassment

What many digital citizens do not realize when they harass their neighbors through digital means, is that they are hurting their own reputation. To their family and friends, an individual who wastes time harassing people online may still be the greatest thing since sliced bread, but to a billion other people, they are going to look like a jerk.

When citizens harass others over a global public platform known as the World Wide Web, they do not just bully their victim, they harass the world. With billions of people interacting online, a bully can never know who will take exception to their remarks.

- Would you walk up to a serial murderer or the relative of a violent criminal or gang member and harass them to their face, or call them a hurtful "four-letter-word?"

Everyone may want to think twice before harassing someone with digital technology: Targeted victims, their friends or their family members could be the next Eric Harris and Dylan Klebold (the shooters behind Columbine) or the next Charles Manson or Ted Bundy (serial killers). Hurtful remarks may just move bullies to the head of a "kill list" — and it is not that hard to find anyone through the Internet.

If citizens author malicious or hurtful messages via digital technology, they are at the helm of the digital device when they draft a malicious message, and *they* are purposefully setting out to publicly harm and or humiliate other individuals using a global public platform. Therefore, *they* are going to have to take the accountability for their actions.

It is incredible how many people in this world will not speak directly to another individual about a problem or issue they have with them, but *will*, behind closed doors, "bravely" confront or "bully" them over the World Wide Web (yeah, there was a bit of sarcasm there).

So why is this happening so frequently in our digital community?

Digital technology offers the ability for instant gratification and physical separation where digital citizens no longer have to "tell someone off" in their minds or wait to tell them to their face. With digital technology, citizens can tell someone off immediately from their desk, car, bed, wherever they are; whether the person they are upset with is around or not. People can lash out at whomever has upset them, just when they are at their angriest and have the most hurtful and malicious things to say. However, as is the case in any life situation, just because citizens *can* does not always mean that they *should*!

A hasty and harsh reaction to events, people and situations using digital technologies opens us up to many very serious issues and circumstances.

We do not have to look far past the following case to see that a real issue we are facing is the ability to *instantly* react.

> "Wayne Treacy, (15), reportedly attacked Josie Ratley on March 17th, 2010 after she allegedly texted him a remark that he didn't like concerning the recent suicide of his older brother." (Olmeda, 2010)

While no one ever deserves to be physically attacked, without digital technology perhaps the "text" that allegedly "set Wayne off" never happens because of the "human filter"; it is much more difficult for many people to make a violent or hurtful comment to someone's face than it is to write it on an (impersonal) digital tool.

Before the ability to instantly vent frustrations via text messages or the World Wide Web, we had a filter. We may have yelled about someone to ourselves or a friend to "cool down" — but once we had a chance to vent, the situation passed, and may never have escalated.

Think about a time when you have been really frustrated at someone. Maybe it was a boss, or a friend, or someone that just cut you off on the road. Keep this moment in your mind, and now let us look at two different scenarios using your situation.

1) **Offline:** If you had no digital technology or the Internet, how would you handle the situation? Would you ever take time out of your day to call everyone in your town or the world to vent about what just happened?

   Before digital technology, if someone made you angry at work, you may have yelled at them from inside your mind, or on the phone to a friend, or at home to a relative, making very harsh comments or judgments. However, those words disappear into thin air. Offline, your co-worker would not hear you ranting, and neither would the rest of the world, so what harm is really being done to your reputation, or theirs.

2) **Digital:** Remembering the same frustrating situation, would you vent everything you thought in your head about the person that frustrated you with your digital technology or the World Wide Web?

Creating malicious or derogatory content about our digital neighbors on a global public platform is an *extremely* irresponsible act, and an egregious example of poor digital judgment because digitally (permanently) documenting anger and frustration does more than bring (potentially) global attention to the circumstance, it paints a picture of the *author* of that malicious content and gives others a negative perception of the citizen who's venting. Moments of anger will pass internally, but the irresponsibility of documenting it via digital technology ensures citizen's hateful words cannot be taken back once their anger subsides. This kind of irresponsibility creates a lasting reputational blemish with potentially negative and haunting Consequences!

All digital citizens, but especially adults, must understand this, as it is our responsibility to explain this to our children. The second someone makes us angry is the second we can voice that opinion through digital technology. We can vent that frustration to the world instantly, but I'll reiterate, just because we *can*, does *not* mean we *should*!

Today, via digital technology we can instantly vent our venom, we can harass or attack immediately without having time to think about what we are doing, and when we act without a Digital Consciousness, we neglect to understand that our reaction is one of permanence and may start a chain reaction of issues that will remain with us and our legacy.

Digital Technology has an infinite number of beneficial uses and conveniences, but attempting to publicly (and globally) damage another individual's reputation or feelings is not one of them. It is time to start using digital tools and technologies the way they are intended to be used — as powerful tools of convenience and constructive communication.

Digital citizens are going to learn the easy way or the hard way to stop misusing digital technology to harass their fellow digital neighbors, and it is my hope they will elect to take the easy way before a malicious message comes back to cost them a job, relationship, education or worse.

You can find more information, thoughts and discussion topics about Digital Harassment in the Appendix under the section titled, "Opinions, Stories and Discussion Topics."

Knowledge In The Neighborhood

Now that we understand that we live in one digital neighborhood, it's time to start looking at how we can function here responsibly and safely. To begin with, we need to change our digital mindset and in doing so we need to understand some common and dangerous misconceptions about our new global village.

It is dangerous to accept as true the widely held beliefs that:

1. We are not totally responsible and accountable for ourselves and what we do and create in a digital world

2. We have true privacy and anonymity in a digital world, and

3. We can simply delete content from a digital device and that will make it "go away."

Let's take a deeper look at each of these 3 misperceptions and replace them with knowledge.

1. We are not totally responsible and accountable for ourselves and what we do and create in a digital world

You Are In Control

Perception: We are not totally responsible and accountable for ourselves and what we do and create in a digital world.

Knowledge: We are not slaves to technology but rather slaves to our own digital ignorance. Everything that we do and create with technology is the result of choices that we make, and it is these choices which determine the positive or negative outcomes that are associated with our digital decisions.

As a society, we must begin to re-evaluate and transform our perceptions into knowledge as we continue using and relying on digital tools and technologies. It is ignorance that leads us to believe that we are nothing more than the helpless victims of technology, of others, of things we can't control — chaos — once we find ourselves in trouble as a result of our own irresponsible or ignorant digital activities (malicious or innocent).

For example, let's say we are shopping online through a reputable, safe and secure store, and we purchase a book. Shortly thereafter, we find out our credit card number was stolen. We believe that we are the victim of digital technology, the store's poor security or a criminal using digital technology. However, if we never installed, updated and ran reputable antivirus *and* antispyware programs on a daily basis, then it wasn't technology's fault that our information was stolen — it was our own. If we employ poor digital decision making and permit malware to exist on our hard drive (which is how our credit card information was stolen), then our information was not taken through the secure store we were shopping at, *we* handed it to a neighbor in our global village through *our* computer, and it is ultimately we who are at fault.

In this scenario, we are quick to blame someone else (i.e. the store, the criminal, technology), all the while taking no accountability for our severe ignorance. We fail to recognize that even though we responsibly used a secure website and entered a secure checkout area, the source of the "information leak" was *our* computer because we failed to do what was necessary on our end to keep the information from becoming accessible to criminals. This would be no different than leaving your wallet on a counter in a crowded market place and expecting nobody to take it. If you leave the wallet, and it is taken or goes missing, who is to blame for the loss? You of course, because you left your wallet behind.

2. We have true privacy and anonymity in a digital world

PRIVA-WHAT?

Perception: We have true privacy and anonymity in a digital world.

Knowledge: Your (digital) privacy is *not* gone; it was *never* there to begin with! Your privacy (digital or otherwise) is completely up to you, and how "private" you are online and offline should remain synonymous.

Belief that there is Absolute privacy or anonymity when using digital tools is a fantastic example of society's misperception about digital technologies, and this is ultimately the catalyst for a myriad of negative Effects — because the mind (the Cause) is flawed.

Where do we hear, read or see the word "privacy" in the phrase World Wide Web?

We throw around the term, "Internet" and we lose focus on the fact that the World Wide Web is a global *public* platform that was designed to *share* thoughts, ideas and information; it was meant for *sharing* information — *not* keeping it "private". The mass assumption that a tool called the World Wide Web should be or "*is*" private is turning out to be one of mankind's greatest and most dangerous misperceptions about technology.

While I cannot force you to truly understand that you have no real privacy in the digital world, I will do my best to help you get past this misperception by providing a few news items and resources (out of tens of thousands I could point you to) that I think illustrate how little privacy we really have.

If you are a parent, you may find this piece to be hair-raising:

> "Echometrix, a leading software company that sells child monitoring programs to parents, crossed the line when it tried to package portions of Internet chats between users it has secretly collected and sell them to third-party advertisers, the New York Attorney General said.
>
> New York-based Echometrix began offering a program last year to marketers interested in learning what people were saying about their products and services online. The program, called Pulse, mined and analyzed recorded conversations stored through the company monitoring software, but it did not tell consumers it was sharing the data." (Koleva, 2010)

If you are behaving in a digital world thinking that you are anonymous or that your activity is "private" then you will want to review this excerpt which talks about major technology providers who have come under fire for sharing customer data with the authorities, and admitting to "spying" abilities that would "shock" and "confuse" customers.

> A CNBC interview with Google CEO Eric Schmidt suggested that users should be wary of what Google knows about them -- and with whom Google can share that information.
>
> CNBC's Mario Bartiromo asked CEO Schmidt in her December 3, 2009 interview: "People are treating Google like their most trusted friend. Should they?"

Schmidt's reply hinted that if there's scandalous information out there about you — it's your problem, not Google's.

Schmidt told Baritoromo:

"If you have something that you don't want anyone to know, maybe you shouldn't be doing it in the first place."

He expanded on his answer, adding that your information could be made available not only to curious searchers or prying friends, but also to the authorities, and that there's little recourse for people worried about unintentionally "oversharing" online:

"But if you really need that kind of privacy, the reality is that search engines, including Google, do retain this information for some time. And [...] we're all subject, in the U.S. to the Patriot Act, and it is possible that that information could be made available to the authorities."

I think the following news item released in September 2010, "Judge Grants Discovery of Postings on Social Media" does a terrific job of illustrating the wisdom and reality of Eric Schmidt's previous two statements:

> A Suffolk County, N.Y. judge ruled that a plaintiff must give a defendant access to private postings from Facebook and MySpace that could contradict claims she made in a personal injury action.
>
> Acting Justice Jeffrey Arlen Spinner of New York's Suffolk County Supreme Court held that precluding defendant Steelcase Inc. from accessing the plaintiff's private postings on Facebook and MySpace "not only would go against the liberal discovery policies of New York favoring pretrial disclosure, but would condone the plaintiff's attempt to hide relevant information behind self-regulated privacy settings."
>
> The judge continued, "In light of the fact that the public portions of the plaintiff's social networking sites contain material that is contrary to her claims and deposition testimony, there is a reasonable likelihood that the private portions of her sites may contain further evidence such as

information with regard to her activities and enjoyment of life, all of which are material and relevant to the defense of this action." (Walder, 2010)

An individual's lack of Digital Consciousness typically means that they subscribe to the illusion that there is Absolute privacy, anonymity and invincibility in a digital world. It is frightening to think that there are millions of people operating digital tools and technologies with these delusions. Negative digital consequences, like those highlighted in Section 4, can be prevented by comprehending that your actions in a digital world are *not* private, and by recognizing that you should *never* create or store any content you would want to keep "private" or "hidden" from anyone else onto a digital device. When you use digital tools and technologies with a transparent manner or mindset — "my actions will be public and permanent" — you operate with a Digital Consciousness.

The Anon Syndrome

If you or anyone you know truly believes that you have anonymity and privacy through the Internet, your cell phone or any other digital tool of communication, then you are setting yourself up for what could potentially be a very dangerous situation. If we truly had anonymity, if we could visit any website (illegal or not), say and do anything we wanted (illegal or not), or take pictures with our cell phones (illegal or not) and be truly "anonymous" (an "anon") like a digital ghost, then why are terrorists not running the globe through Facebook or YouTube?

When looking at it from the perspective of keeping "terrorists" from frequently and anonymously executing their agendas through digital technology, perhaps we not only realize that we don't truly have Absolute privacy or anonymity, but that we (because terrorists would have it too) don't want it!

The fact is, the only thing keeping tens of thousands of people out of jail is a lack of human resources. There just isn't enough man power to investigate, arrest and prosecute all of the individuals in the global village that think (with or without a proxy) they are anonymously:

- Making a violent threat
- Digitally extorting and blackmailing their digital neighbors

- Looking at sexually explicit content of minors on the Internet
- Inappropriately communicating with underage citizens via digital tools

Think about this hypothetical scenario: If you were king or queen for a year, and you had supreme rule — you could do whatever you wanted with no repercussions or payback, would you ever mass distribute any tool that could be used to over throw or usurp your power?

Most people I ask that question to say (quite loudly), "NO!"

This answer makes perfect sense as an individual or group in power is not (typically) going to willingly give it up to someone else. This is exactly why no government or organization on this planet will ever (legally) permit the mass distribution of any tool (digital or otherwise) to men, women, children and criminals, if there was no way to monitor and control that tool. Why would government permit the (legal) dissemination of a digital tool, Internet browser tool, application or proxy that would allow a citizen to be Absolutely "dark" or "anonymous?" It is ignorant to think that any citizen in general society would ever be in control of the latest and most powerful digital technologies.

Ask yourself this question, "What do I use my digital tools for?"

When I ask people across the United States how and why they use their digital tools, I typically receive the following responses:

- To talk or text with my friends
- To communicate with my family
- To get news
- To get directions
- To watch media
- For research

These examples illustrate the intended use and benefits of digital technology. They illustrate that digital tools are being used by citizens for many of the purposes they are intended to be used for — to share and find information as well as (instantly) communicate — not for privacy! Almost every digital issue that surfaces in the news and in our communities stems from an individual or group that uses their technology assuming what they are doing will remain anonymous or private.

If you are an individual that thinks your are digitally anonymous, open up an internet browser, go to your favorite search engine, and perform a search for an article titled, *"The case that could end cyberbullying."* What you will learn is that, in October, 2010 Google was ordered by a New York judge to reveal the identity of an "anonymous" user who was bullying a woman on YouTube. After reviewing this article, you may begin to realize that you may not be as anonymous as you think.

In my humble opinion, increased public and media attention to cases like this will help to dispel the myth of anonymity in a digital world, which will significantly reduce the number of bullying incidents in the global village as the number of cowards who are only willing to "bully" while trying to hide behind digital technology, will realize that there is actually nowhere to hide.

Honest Scott

In 1999, Scott McNealy, co founder, (then) Chief Executive Officer of Sun Microsystems made this statement in the press: "You have zero privacy anyway, so get over it". (PCWorld, 2000) Scott was panned by many media outlets and organizations when, in my humble opinion, he should have been placed on a pedestal for honesty.

Why?

Because it was the truth, and knowing the potential consequences of making a statement like that in the press, he was honest with our society who should be, but clearly is not, listening.

I constantly receive questions such as:

- "What if my Facebook account is hacked?"
- "What if my cell phone is hacked?"
- "How is it right or legal that there were websites like pleaserobme.com that listed status updates showing posts of people twittering they are not home?"
- "What about my privacy?"

My response to these questions is typically to ask:

> *"Would any of these concerns matter to you if there was no content in your Facebook account, or on your cell phone that could be taken and used against you? Who cares if your Facebook or cell phone content is stolen if there is nothing exploitable to be used against you? Who cares if your Facebook or cell phone content is stolen if there is nothing more on it than a picture of your dog, a funny joke or commentary on your favorite television series?*
>
> *In terms of a website like twitter or foursquare.com that compiles and share people's status updates and locations — often times telling us when people are not home — I ask you, what content or "leads" would a criminal have to use to rob anyone or stalk anyone if digital citizens realized that you should never post a current or future status update on something called the World Wide Web?*
>
> *The real question we must ask ourselves is, "why would I ever place or say anything on an Internet connected digital tool that I would not want the world to see?" If your answer is, I wouldn't, then you have a Digital Consciousness."*

"Passwords" or "Passing-Right-Through Words"

Understand that "passwords" (on unsecured web sites) are a joke to many hackers and criminals. Passwords provide us with the *illusion* of privacy, of protection, but at the end of the day, our passwords can literally be brushed aside like a curtain. Passwords are not the "steel doors" many believe they are. Think about it like this: Why would there even be a word called "hacking" if passwords were so secure? How could anyone "hack" an account if passwords were impenetrable? If we couldn't illegally access an account, a page, a password, something that is supposed to be "private," then we would never need a reason to label the act of illegally accessing an account, with the word "hacking," right?

The truth of the matter is that hacking exists because the action of hacking is very possible. It occurs much more often than most people want to realize. Ever hear of Firesheep? Go ahead and try a search on your favorite search engine for the term "Firesheep application." What you will learn is that Firesheep is a web plug-in that helps citizens access other people's online accounts (like Facebook and Twitter) over the same wireless network. Do you think this will be the last application that will ever be developed to help people hack accounts now that this "box" as been opened? With this in mind, *never* place information on an unsecure website thinking that a password is going to keep everyone out.

Note: For a site to be secure, it should offer the following:

- The URL in the address bar begins with "http**s**" — without the "**s**" it is not secure.

- An icon of a closed padlock should be visible somewhere in the browser window. If you click on the padlock, you should see information about the site's security certificate.

- Secure sites will typically display a prominent image depicting a certificate seal on their website. Sometimes clicking on this image will also provide information about the site's security certificate.

To illustrate a point, go ahead and try an Internet search for "how to hack websites" and take a look at the results you get. I will warn you however, that clicking into sites offering information and services about hacking are frequently scams set up to steal your money, identity, or worse, and could present some significant security issues for you. If you try to work with organizations in the digital black market, you better be prepared to encounter a variety of dangers because you don't get to make a deal with the devil and walk away "clean." Therefore, I will reiterate that I highly recommend you do not click into or use any services provided for hacking. This exercise is suggested merely to illustrate how many search results and services offer to help people hack social media accounts (such as Facebook, YouTube and others). The truth is, there are a lot of people that want to hack into sites and they can. I think that the following excerpt from, "Researchers show new way to hack social networking sites" helps hammer this point home:

> Researchers have found a new technique that cyber-criminals could exploit to steal users' credentials.
>
> At a Black Hat computer security conference in Las Vegas, researchers demonstrated software they developed that could steal online credentials from users of popular websites such as Facebook, eBay and Google.

> The attack relies on a new type of hybrid file that looks like different things to different programs. By placing these files on sites that allow users to upload their own images, the researchers can circumvent security systems and take over the accounts of web surfers who use these sites. (McMillan, 2008)

Remember, there will always be new individuals, organizations and systems working to hack an account, even though many hacker solutions will be thwarted. Digital citizens should never ask the question:

"What happens if someone hacks my Facebook account and steals my pictures?"

The question should always be:

"Why would I care?"

Look at it this way: Who cares if somebody takes pictures out of your account if you are not uploading content that can be used to exploit you — if you are OK with everything you upload becoming public and permanent!

So how did society become so misinformed about privacy?

Much of it has to do with assumption. For example:

- Some people believe that when sitting alone in their rooms with their computers, nobody can see what is on their Internet-connected computers or the websites they visit.

- Some believe that if they send a picture or text message to friends via a cell phone, only their friends can see it.

- Some people have a mindset that they own their personal web page (i.e. Facebook page), and that their passwords are protecting their content and account from "strangers."

If these thoughts and assumptions sound familiar to you, then I am very happy that you are reading this guide.

Unfortunately our society has been flooded with misinformation and half-truths regarding digital privacy and security. For example, when an *unsecure* (social networking) website launches press notifying the public that they have made updates to their privacy settings, they paint a picture of corporate and social responsibility in an attempt to position themselves as a network working to assist the greater good. Often times however, all that this press is ultimately designed to do is garner more web site attention, unique users, traffic and content for their service and platform. In these cases, the press releases are only for *the company* as their users don't really have privacy to begin with, and the website developers know this. Obviously they don't become a top website without knowing what they are doing, and by publicizing updated privacy settings, websites are providing dangerous misinformation to the public in hopes of garnering greater web traffic and positive PR from individuals that lack a Digital Consciousness.

For example, a press release that publicizes "updated privacy settings" can falsely imply that there is Absolute privacy on an unsecure social website that sits on the World Wide Web. This press release ultimately communicates to many in our digital world a false sense of security. It makes many users feel comfortable loading all kinds of personal information onto their "personal" page increasing the website's traffic, user base, content and most importantly each individual's personal risk. Believing there is true privacy opens the flood gates for uploading "private pictures", status updates, personal information like phone numbers, home and school addresses and more onto a global public platform that we would typically not tell a total stranger at the local park.

Let's take a look at a real example of what I am talking about. Think about this, how many times just in the first half of 2010 did we see the words "privacy" and "Facebook" in a headline. How many times did we see industry "experts" reacting to issues and discussing the privacy — or lack thereof — on this platform? Not surprisingly however — as is the case with many websites — it appears that privacy concerns were understood by Facebook's developers long before concerns began popping up the media.

According to Business Insider SAI sources, the following exchange occurred between a 19-year-old Mark Zuckerberg and a friend shortly after Mark launched The Facebook in his dorm room. (Carlson, 2010)

> Zuck: Yeah so if you ever need info about anyone at Harvard
>
> Zuck: Just ask.
>
> Zuck: I have over 4,000 emails, pictures, addresses, SNS

[Redacted Friend's Name]: What? How'd you manage that one?

Zuck: People just submitted it.

Zuck: I don't know why.

Zuck: They "trust me"

Zuck: Dumb f*cks. (Carlson, 2010)

Despite your interpretation of these comments, it is clear that even Mark was surprised by the irresponsibility of the users on his platform as he indicated when he said, *"people just submitted it, I don't' know why"*. In my humble opinion, if Mark (and this applies to a number of other website owners and managers) was upfront and honest like Scott McNealy when Facebook first launched, he could have proactively saved himself and his company a great deal of grief *if* he had just said something similar to, *"hey, please remember that you are posting your information on a shared global public platform that rests on the World Wide Web and is used by billions of people who can, and will, do whatever they want with the information you are posting."*

If (unsecure) social websites truly wanted to *enhance* your security and privacy settings, they would encrypt your account like a reputable online bank, or be honest and communicate accurate information such as, *"This unsecured website offers you no real privacy as it exists on the World Wide Web. Therefore, you should not post any information you are uncomfortable sharing with a world of strangers."*

> **Note:** I want to be clear that I use and enjoy Facebook, and I am not trying to dissuade your use of this site or discredit this social network in any way. I am hard pressed to find an unsecure interactive or social website that makes it visibly clear to their users that their *unsecured website offers you no real privacy as it exists on the World Wide Web, and thus, you should not post any information you are uncomfortable sharing with a world of strangers.* Facebook is one of the world's largest social sites, and therefore is going to garner more (press) attention and, like an older sibling, is looked upon to set an appropriate example or industry standard.

Updated privacy settings can fill us with a sense of privacy and security. However, as you continue on your course to Digital Consciousness, you will not only realize that privacy is an illusion on a global public platform called the World Wide Web, but you will also learn the serious risks of posting the aforementioned type of information to a global platform.

The Blame Game

So who is to blame for the myth of privacy in a digital world?

Obviously, based on our previous example I believe that website developers need to assume some responsibility for the way in which they are marketing Internet privacy to their consumers. However, when people post information that they don't want the world to see on a third-party site, such as Facebook, should Facebook be held accountable if a criminal sees — and perhaps uses — that content? Absolutely not — the person who posted the information should be!

In fact, as our example has shown, even the creator of Facebook couldn't believe the lax attitude that everyday citizens had when it came to sharing personal information on his website. At the time of the platform's launch, it seemed crazy that his classmates would just post personal information to a public platform and "trust" him with the information. With that being said, doesn't it seem even *crazier* today that an entire society of individuals including teachers, students, parents, executives, law enforcement, government officials and more across the globe would ever post "personal" or "private" information on a public global platform full of strangers? To this end, if websites wanted media, experts, organizations and citizens to stop "coming down" on them for privacy issues, they should place all the accountability where it belongs — on the user.

> **Web Hosting Tip:** For anyone that owns an unsecure website, or is thinking about starting an unsecure website, *now* is as good a time as any to update your privacy policy so the bigger and better your website gets, the less accountability you and the site will incur. Ensure that responsible use of your website completely falls on the user, where it ultimately belongs.
>
> No current or future website can:

- *Make* anyone use their site
- *Make* anyone type in personal information
- *Make* anyone upload a picture to their platform
- *Make* anyone harass somebody via their messaging systems

But a website *can* make us believe that our actions are "private" — and *that* is where they seem to be incurring some responsibility and liability.

Digital Privacy and You

Why do we think we are different people or that we can behave differently with a computer or cell phone than we would on a stage in front of our friends (who can quickly become our enemies), or our spouse (who can quickly become our ex-spouse)?

What type of information do you share online? Think about every word, image and video you have ever posted on a digital device or the World Wide Web. Would you say, show or play these words, images and videos on a stage in front of everyone you have ever known? Would you be OK sharing this information with a room of criminals or a stranger at the park?

If we would not share this content on a stage in front of friends, a room of criminals, or a stranger at the park, then why would we post it to the World Wide Web — the bulletin board for the global village? This is what we must all understand, so we can teach future generations to become responsible citizens online — just as we teach them to be responsible citizens offline.

What is terrifying is the number of individuals standing in front of web cameras, or posting images or videos to the Internet, prefacing their actions with, "this is for your eyes only." Unfortunately, there is no such thing as "for your eyes only" when using the World Wide Web, it is "for the world only!"

Even more incredible is how many individuals will do or say something in front of a digital camera such as flash their "private parts", or make hateful comments, but *before* they do, they look around to make sure nobody is watching, to make sure mom or dad is not in the room. They lock the doors or pull the shades. Then they pull up their shirt lightning fast and put it down again. What is horrifically insane about these preparatory actions, is that these individuals make preparations to try and keep what they are about to do "private", meanwhile, they "do it" for everyone on the World Wide Web.

There are far too many digital citizens that Truly think what they are doing in front of a web camera, digital (video) camera, on Skype, etc, will remain "private." Meanwhile, millions of people in the world are watching them and laughing at them *as* they first lock the door or look around the room to be sure nobody is watching, and then take off their clothes, quickly flash the web camera, make a hate filled remark or proceed to make a sexy video for a loved one. The dangerous lack of Digital Consciousness in these individuals is obvious the *second* they take *any* action to try and maintain "privacy" for what they are about to do, because they do not realize that their actions may be public and permanent for the global village momentarily. The real dangers of this ignorance and how it transforms into exploitation will become clearer in section 4, but for now let's take a look at a couple of quick examples:

> Phillip Sherman of Arkansas learned to hold onto his cell phone the hard way. He left his phone behind at a McDonald's restaurant and nude photos of his wife stored on his phone ended up online. He and his wife, Tina, sued McDonald's Corp., the franchise owner and the store manager seeking a jury trial and $3 million in damages for suffering, embarrassment and the cost of having to move to a new home because of the incident. (The Huffington Post, 2008)

In my humble opinion, we can all thank goodness McDonalds won this case, because if they lost, you can bet your bottom dollar there would be restaurants and other businesses printing up new door signs that say, "no cell phones allowed in this establishment." But why should all citizens have to be inconvienienced for this couple's irresponsibility?

Here is another example of citizens thinking their digital actions were private:

> Nazril Irham was detained over sex tapes that have been circulating online. The singer could face jail time if found guilty of violating Indonesia's strict anti-pornography law. Two

> separate videos allegedly showing the 28-year-old in bed - in each, with a different celebrity girlfriend - started circulating on the Internet in early June 2010. Local media said the video started appearing in early June after Irham's laptop was stolen and many similar tapes, with other celebrities, were still out there. (Martinez, 2010)

Here is an example of the consequences that befell some individuals that stood in front of their web cameras not realizing — whether they pulled their shades or locked their doors — that they were being recorded for the digital world to see:

> "A Massachusetts man in his 40s stands accused of posing as a 17-year old boy so he could lure teenage girls into video chatrooms and secretly videotape them as they engaged in sexual acts. According to documents filed in federal court in Los Angeles, the man harvested pictures from an unknown boy's MySpace account and set up fictitious accounts such as this on the social networking site Stickam. He allegedly befriended girls and encouraged them to perform sexual acts in private video chat rooms. "Although the Victim believed she was performing privately for her 17-year-old online boyfriend, a video recording of the Victim masturbating for Silipigni has surfaced on the Internet," an FBI agent wrote in an affidavit that was filed, about an unidentified 14-year-old girl from California. In all, Silipigni collected about 100 videos from underage girls he tricked under the guise." (Goodin, 2009)

I could provide you with more examples than you could read in a lifetime as every day there are thousands more just like these. This information really hits home at the IROC2 Live Events as audiences at these events can visually see the Effects and Consequences I am describing here. Real visual-aids and live (online) examples illustrate what happens to many people that do things with digital technology they would not do "on stage" in front of friends, family and enemies. There are too many digital citizens who have no idea that their "private" or "for you only" pictures and videos or web cam sessions are actually content for pornographic websites that steal and use this content to minimize start up and operational costs (this is further illustrated in Section 4).

"For your eyes only" is misperception; "for the world only" is knowledge – It is all fun and games until someone (else) uses an eye!

Remember, *you* are your own privacy filter, *not* a cell phone carrier or website's "privacy settings."

Viruses and Spyware and Phishing, Oh My

For the same reason you take vitamins to boost your immune system, for the same reason you lock your doors to keep strangers out, you absolutely *must* continuously update and run antivirus and anti spyware programs daily. Further, you need to occasionally run those same programs in Safe Mode.

It is astounding how few technology users are familiar with what computer viruses, spyware and phishing are. Using technology, especially the Internet and smart phones, and not knowing what these types of malicious programs are is like walking through a school, workplace or town and not knowing what a cold or flu is and how you can be infected.

Every user of digital technology should be just as vigilant and preventative (not reactive) towards maintaining immunity from computer viruses and spyware (often called malware) as we are when it comes to avoiding biological viruses such as the flu.

Let's first define computer viruses, spyware programs and phishing to eliminate confusion beyond this point. Of course there are always slight variations depending on the source, but the following definitions from Microsoft® do a fine job of defining these malicious forms of malware:

> **Computer Virus:** "Computer viruses are small software programs that are designed to spread from one computer to another and to interfere with computer operation.
>
> A virus might corrupt or delete data on your computer, use your e-mail program to spread itself to other computers, or even erase everything on your hard disk. Computer viruses are often spread by attachments in e-mail messages or instant messaging messages. That is why it is essential that you never open e-mail attachments unless you know who it's from and you are expecting it. Viruses can be disguised as attachments

of funny images, greeting cards, or audio and video files. Computer viruses also spread through downloads on the Internet. They can be hidden in illicit software or other files or programs you might download.

To help avoid computer viruses, it's essential that you keep your computer current with the latest updates and antivirus tools, stay informed about recent threats, run your computer as a standard user (not as administrator), and that you follow a few basic rules when you surf the Internet, download files, and open attachments. Once a virus is on your computer, its type or the method it used to get there is not as important as removing it and preventing further infection." (Microsoft Corporation®)

Spyware: "Spyware is software that can install itself or run on your computer without providing you with adequate notice, consent, or control. Spyware might not display symptoms after it infects your computer, but many types of malicious software or unwanted programs can affect how your computer runs. Spyware can, for example, monitor your online behavior or collect information about you (including personally identifiable or other sensitive information), change settings on your computer, or cause your computer to run slowly." (Microsoft Corporation®)

Phishing: "Online phishing (pronounced like the word fishing) is a way to trick computer users into revealing personal or financial information through a fraudulent e-mail message or website. A common online phishing scam starts with an e-mail message that looks like an official notice from a trusted source, such as a bank, credit card company, or reputable online merchant. In the e-mail message, recipients are directed to a fraudulent website where they are asked to provide personal information, such as an account number or password. This information is then usually used for identity theft." (Microsoft Corporation®)

Now that we have defined these major forms of malware (there are millions of variations), you may more clearly understand the impact they can have should you become infected, and how poor digital judgment combined with an "infection" can result in severe Consequences. For example, perhaps you have sensitive financial data or you have loaded some "sexy pictures" of yourself or someone else onto your computer's hard drive. If your computer is infected with spyware, those pictures, along with any other data on that hard drive is "exposed" and is accessible by the third party or criminal behind the spyware. Making matters even worse is the way you may find out that a criminal has seen, or is using your "private" content (as further explained in section 4).

In case you think this is a farfetched idea, here is an actual news item for you to consider:

> "According to the Department of Justice Press Release from June 22, 2010, Luis Mijangos of Santa Ana, California hacked into a victim's computer and turn on the computer's webcam once in awhile, hoping to film his female victims in compromising situations. If he did so, he blackmailed her with the footage, basically an involuntarily made sex tape, threatening to make it public if she did not send him more explicit videos. He also blackmailed his victims with photos or videos he found on their hardrives. According to the FBI report, he looked specifically for images of young women and girls in various states of undress or engaged in sexual acts with their partners. He threaten[ed] to distribute those stolen images and videos to every addressee in the victims' contact lists unless they made additional videos for him. He tried to keep his victims from reporting him to the police by telling them that because he controlled their computer, he would know if they went to the authorities." (Levinson, 2010)

Just in case that story isn't enough to raise your level of concern, here is a story about phishing that was shared with me after a Live Event in New Hampshire.

> A school official was shopping online for a reputable antivirus program on his lunch break at school. He performed a search for the software he desired and then clicked a link in his search results which took him to what looked like his preferred Antivirus' website. After a few minutes, he was finished with

his transaction which seemed to be a very easy and user friendly process. After a few more minutes, he became concerned that he did not receive an email with a receipt, a download link or any other confirmation of his purchase. Shortly thereafter however, he did receive a phone call. It was from the school's "IT" department alerting him that the schools network was infected with malware. Not too long after this situation, he realized his credit card was being used fraudulently, and ultimately, his identity was stolen.

So how did this happen?

The website he was directed to looked like the official website for the antivirus company he sought, *but* it was located at a URL that was not affiliated with the antivirus company. Phishing sites can employ subtle changes in the web address such as using a capital "i" ("I") in place of a lowercase "L" ("l") or by using a Zero in place of the letter "O" because these symbols are interchangeable. As such, you must *always* check the URL bar closely and be sure it is the correct website, and always make sure it is secure when you check out!

Now that I've bombarded you with everything you'd ever want to know about phishing, here is some information about Remote Access Trojans (RATS) for you to consider. While you're reading this section, keep in mind that it is programs like these, *combined* with society's ignorance to them *and* poor digital decisions, that make identity theft and exploitation top crimes in our global village.

RATS – Remote Access Trojans – can control your computer. Criminals can use this technique to expose you to scams because RAT programs can trick your computer into thinking that a site is trust-worthy, or they can mimic your online banking, shopping or other sites that you frequently visit. The criminal can then use your passwords or credit card numbers to steal your money and/or identity. Remote Access Trojans can view, alter, copy, and/or delete your files from your computer, turn your webcam on and off without your knowledge, and cause your system to function improperly or crash completely. RATS record your activity and send the information to another computer allowing criminals to gain access to your user names, passwords and other personal information. These programs can also capture video and audio from any devices that you have hooked up to your computer. Remote Access Trojans are also capable of running and/or ending any processes, programs, or connections you have on your computer, and can create pop-ups to annoy you or get you to go to malicious web sites.

The fact is, RATS are just *one* example of how malicious a malware program can be which is why it is so very important that you do everything you can to proactively protect your computer and yourself, just as you would do to prevent any biological disease.

Protecting Yourself and Your Data

Now that we know the dangers involved with ignoring viruses and spyware, what can we do to prevent them?

Well, just like with biological diseases, we have a choice when faced with digital viruses and spyware. We can either choose to be reactive and try to minimize the impact of every virus that infects us, or we can be proactive and take steps to prevent infection all together. For a clearer example, think about this in terms of the following scenarios:

> With a *reactive* approach in a digital world, should you be infected, it is probable that the Consequences could amount to your personal information, content, and potentially your identity being stolen. In fact, according to Symantec, as of June 28, 2010, an identity is stolen every 3 seconds online, and 1 in 5 people is the victim of cyber crime. (Symantec Corporation)

> With a *proactive* approach, in a digital world, you would be continuously (auto) updating and (auto) running your antivirus and antispyware programs. You could minimize your risk of falling victim to scams and phishing sites, preventing the agonizing and frustrating reactionary measures involved in curing a [digital] infection.

Now, does a proactive approach mean that your antimalware programs will always catch *every* virus or spyware program? Of course not just as washing your hands or taking your vitamins every day will not fend off *every* infection. However, it absolutely minimizes the chances of the most malicious programs infecting you and more importantly, existing for an extended period of time on your machine. Remember that just as we use a proactive approach or Health Consciousness to avoid biological infections, we should be using the same proactive approach to avoid digital infections.

For more information about reputable antivirus and antispyware programs, you can contact the Office of the Cyber General through The Institute for Responsible Online and Cell-Phone Communication.

3. We can simply delete content from a digital device and that will make it "go away."

Deleting & Recovering Content

Perception: We can simply delete content from a digital device and that will make it "go away."

Knowledge: Simply hitting the delete button does not make content "disappear."

Are you a user of digital technology that believes deleting something from your digital tool's memory (the computer, cell phone or digital camera) truly deletes it? Makes it unrecoverable? Well if so then I have some news for you. The idea that simply hitting the "delete" button will make your content disappear is a mass misperception that blurs our lens of digital knowledge.

Think about this for a moment: If you were abducted and law enforcement believed that a lead to your recovery had been deleted from your computer's hard drive, your cell phone or your Facebook page, wouldn't you want them to have a way to "recover" that information in hopes it would lead to your rescue?

Fortunately for you and me and all of us, this is possible, because a simple push of the delete button, does not mean delete, destroy or disintegrate. The fact is, what you delete, by pressing the "delete" button is actually not deleting the content at all.

Let's look at what actually happens when you think you are deleting content from:

- Your computer's hard drive,
- Your cell phone, digital camera or other digital device's memory cards, and
- The World Wide Web

Your Computer's Brilliant Memory

Imagine you just finished a 20 page research proposal, or you just loaded 2 days of vacation pictures to your computer's hard drive, and then, while celebrating your accomplishment you accidentally deleted the information or files. Ouch! While many people would be quite upset, there are millions of citizens with a Digital Consciousness that realize this is not really a major issue because deleting a file from your hard drive, doesn't really delete it. Now, this is extremely righteous news if you need to "recover" a paper or the 2 days of vacation pictures you could never replicate, but this could also be disturbing news if you have been abusing your computer by doing "naughty" or illegal things and thought that you could hide your activity and content with the "delete" button.

Many people realize that deleted files, folders and other forms of computer data get sent to your Recycle Bin as a backup that allows you to quickly and easily "un-delete" a file that you want to restore. However, what many citizens do not realize is that when the information is emptied from their Recycle Bin, it has not really been deleted or vaporized into oblivion. The fact is, the successful recovery of the files you empty from your Recycle Bin can be accomplished quite easily through a variety of programs and methods. In other words, just because you empty your recycle bin does not mean that the files you thought you got rid of are actually gone.

How is this possible?

When you empty your recycle bin, only the *path* to where those files are located on your system have been removed, but the information you deleted is still within your hard drive. Just because the computer does not recognize that the "deleted" files are still within your computer's memory does *not* mean they no longer exist. This is the reason that the recovery of what many believe to be "deleted" data can be easily accomplished; because it was never actually removed or "deleted" to begin with.

Now knowing this, imagine you lose, sell or throw away your computer without removing the hard drive, and someone "less than altruistic" winds up with it. They could install a "hard drive recovery program" onto your computer, and essentially un-delete files that you believed were deleted. This opens the door for them to obtain financial data, "private" pictures and other exploitable material for use on the digital black market. This is why it is always a good idea to remove and destroy the hard drive before getting rid of your computer.

Remember, by itself your computer cannot upload anything harmful. Only you can load sexy pictures, hateful remarks, or leave a trail of "dark" web activity that another person might find. Further, your computer cannot install antivirus and antispyware programs by itself, thus, should you not be vigilant with your computer's health and security, *some* of the accountability for the theft of any private information through spyware rests on your shoulders! After all, if you never washed your hands, showered, or practiced a general Health Consciousness, you would have to take some accountability if you got sick, no?

A frequent comment I receive at Live Events is:

"I can format my hard drive or run a kill disk program to reduce the chances of recovery."

Sure you can, but are you willing to do this right now? Would you put this book down and go format and "kill" your hard drive this instant? What about *right* after you do something you don't want to "come back?" Would you format your hard drive every single time you "deleted" any file?

If you are not willing to format your hard drive every time you delete any file, then this comment is pointless. This comment is even more ignorant if your hard drive is stolen, lost, hacked or seized by law enforcement because in each of these scenarios, you do not even have the hard drive in your possession to format or "kill." Trying to format or kill your hard drive *after* you have a problem usually means you are too late.

For more information about hard drive recovery programs, just search for "hard drive recovery programs" on your preferred search engine or contact The Institute for Responsible Online and Cell-Phone Communication on how to find reputable programs.

Remember Me Cards

The following information applies to any digital device that uses a memory card to store content such as a cell phone, digital (video) camera, MP3 player and so on. Understand that, like "deleting" content from a computer, when you delete content from your media, memory or "SIM" card, you are not really "deleting" it from existence. Just because you press delete on your digital camera or cell phone, does NOT mean that what you deleted cannot be recovered. Now, if a situation arose where you wanted to recover vacation pictures that you accidentally deleted, this is most excellent news. But if you were trying to "get rid of the evidence" by simply deleting your pictures or videos from your memory card, this news may be startling and even disturbing.

While many digital tools provide a "delete" feature that enable you to remove pictures and files from your memory card, what many people just do not understand due to a severe lack of Digital Consciousness, is that these files are not actually removed or "deleted" from the memory card. Using very easy to find software available for free online, anyone could recover pictures or files from a memory card that were thought to be erased. These recovery programs are great tools for those who accidentally delete a picture and want to recover it, but can be a terrifying notion for someone who lends their camera out or loses their device with "deleted" pictures that they assume were gone forever.

For instance:

> My son dropped our digital camera in a fountain, and we thought we lost a couple of days worth of pictures because when I pulled the memory card out of the camera, and re-inserted it into another (dry) camera, the card said "corrupt" and there were no pictures visible or available.
>
> Now there are many digital users who would believe that those pictures were gone, and perhaps would even throw that memory card away thinking that this was a terrible situation, and a "lost cause."
>
> Fortunately, I knew that just because it "appeared" the content was missing from the card, it did not mean that it was actually gone. After inserting the card into an external card reader

and running a reputable recovery program, within minutes our family had all of our pictures back (and my son who was feeling pretty bad at the time, had a huge smile on his face). Now, as we sat there and watched the vacation pictures "come back" from this once corrupt card, so did hundreds of other pictures that were "deleted" prior to the vacation. Fortunately, while I was sitting there with my son watching all of these "deleted" pictures come back, I was not nervous that a picture might come back to haunt me or embarrass me in front of my son.

Why?

Because I have a Digital Consciousness; I have a mindset that my digital activity can very quickly become public and permanent, and therefore, I never placed anything on that media card that I would not want my son or anyone else who may have extracted the camera from the water to see, should we have failed to rescue it.

Now let's say for instance that I didn't have a Digital Consciousness. Let's say, for example, that I had a picture on that camera card that I would never want the world, nor my children or grandchildren to see, and I had deleted it a few days prior to that vacation. Let's call this deleted picture, "Picture X." Here are just a couple ways that the picture I thought was deleted, could be seen by the world:

> Scenario 1: I see the memory card is corrupt, so I throw it away. Someone finds it in the trash, takes it out of the trash to save some money or to be nosy, runs a recovery program, and BOOM, they now have the "Picture X" I thought I deleted, and I thought the world would never see. Now I am at this stranger's mercy hoping that they will never show anyone. Yikes!

> Scenario 2: I lose my camera at a restaurant, amusement park, wherever. Someone finds it, runs a recovery program, and BOOM, they now have the "Picture X" I thought I deleted, and I thought the world would never see. Now I am at this stranger's mercy hoping that they will never show anyone. Yikes!

> Scenario 3: I sell my camera at a garage sale or via the Internet, but I don't take the memory card out. The purchaser runs a recovery program, and BOOM…I think you get it by now.
>
> Scenario 4: I plug my camera card into my (Internet-connected) computer and a criminal has spyware on my machine that allows them to see, capture, "undelete" and steal my camera card's content and BOOM…yeah, same awful ending here.

You may be surprised to learn that these scenarios I have provided are not fictional, and they highlight the reason why all of us must maintain a mindset that what we do digitally is public and permanent. "Picture X" *is* fictional, but these examples about how it could get out — these situations all really happened to your neighbors! Each of these four scenarios all come from stories told to me by digital citizens from across the United States from March 2009 through May 2010. I could write pages of examples illustrating the myriad of ways deleted content gets out, but I think you get the point by now.

Ok, I couldn't resist the chance to give you one more story but only because this one surprised even me.

> This story comes from a trade show I attended. A reporter had numerous pictures of an accident for a story on her digital camera card, but the camera card read "corrupt" every time she plugged it into her reader. Both the editor and photographer for the publication were quite upset as they thought the photos for their story were gone.
>
> When they saw that the IROC2.org booth at the expo was about digital technology they requested my assistance. Long story short, within only a few minutes, I was able to "pull back" all of the pictures of the accident that they *thought* were lost when the card read "corrupt."
>
> Unfortunately that is not all that came back. Almost 1,500 pictures were recovered in total, and some of them were images of kids and their friends playing drinking games. Images that were previously deleted before the kids gave their mom her camera for work.

Now think about this:

- When they took those pictures, did those kids think that some guy from New Jersey would ever see their drinking exploits?

- Did they ever think that their mom would see them?

Chances are, the answer to both of these questions is no. However, if they had the mindset that their digital activity would be public and permanent, then maybe they wouldn't have digitally documented their activity.

Now if I was a criminal I could have (*but did not)* easily saved those images to my computer and used them to exploit that publication or that family — especially if those kids were under the age of 21 which they appeared to be — and the mystery for those kids who obviously did not have a Digital Consciousness would have been, "how did those pictures get out?"

At least if they possessed a Digital Consciousness they would have had the opportunity to evaluate the risk vs. the reward of taking those pictures because they would have had a mindset and understanding that their pictures *could* become public and permanent at any time. This is just one of millions of random and obscure ways "private" content gets out.

Remember, if *you* take a picture you would not want the world to see, and it "gets out," it is *you* who is accountable for the consequences, not the camera, not the memory card, not digital technology.

Self Assessment Tip: If you are going to leave your house with any digital tool whether it be a digital camera, cell phone, MP3 player, whatever (I stress cell phones and digital cameras due to their smaller size), then you should be willing to hand that digital tool to anybody, at any time whether it be a friend, family member, stranger or criminal, and let them look at the memory card and let them recover or "un-delete" the memory card right in front of you.

If you are willing to walk out of your home with *any* digital tool, but you would *not* willingly let anybody, at *any* time inspect and recover your memory card, then you are abusing digital technology, and you lack a Digital Consciousness.

Why do I stress this concept so strongly?

Because at any moment, you are literally one second away from losing that device. You are one second from leaving it on a table, having it fall out of your pocket, dropping it in a public place where you cannot retain it and in that one second, BOOM, everything that is, or was, on that device's memory card is now in the hands of someone who may decide to show it to the world!

While we're on the subject, keep in mind that there are also countless ways your device could be stolen or even hacked which exponentially increases your risk.

So remember, if you are going to leave your home with your digital tools, you should be willing to show all (past and current) content on that device to a stranger at any time. If you are not willing to do this, then you are abusing that tool, because you are just a moment away from losing it — setting yourself up for a difficult challenge!

The Bulletin Board of the Global Village – The World Wide Web

There are billions of people on the World Wide Web and the second you post anything online, you are posting information to a bulletin board in the global village. Hopefully by now, you realize that your privacy is nothing more than a dangerous misperception. Understand that once you post that content or information, anyone can save it, screenshot it, share it, or print it making it virtually impossible for the content to really ever be truly deleted. Deleting something from what you perceive as your web page on Facebook, My Space, wherever, does not mean it immediately comes off that platform's servers, and does not delete it from the hard drives of anyone who saved it before you hit delete.

You must understand that you do not "own" your "personal page" on Facebook, MySpace or on any other free third-party platform. You do not pay for your page and you do not host your page. The platform you are using is simply handing you "free space" and you are using their servers, their "real estate" in the global village. The content and space you are using resides on their servers, and therefore, individuals with access to those servers have the ability to look at it, copy it, or even share it.

If you truly believe that some individuals at the websites you use don't "sneak a peek" at what you are posting, let me enlighten you with a direct quote from an employee at Facebook:

> *"When I first started working there, yes — I used it to view other people's profiles which I didn't have permission to visit. I never manipulated their data in any way; however, I did abuse the profile viewing permission at several initial points when I started at Facebook. Your messages are stored in a database, whether deleted or not. So we can just query the database, and easily look at it without ever logging into your account. That's what most people don't understand."* (Tate, 2010)

Did you know that if you "tweet" through Twitter you are likely to be documented in the Library of Congress? Check this out:

> "Every 140-character snippet of info you've ever shared publicly on Twitter will soon have a home next to the Declaration of Independence. Twitter and the Library of Congress announced that every public tweet posted since Twitter started in 2006 will be archived digitally by the Federal Library. The purpose, according to a blog post by Library of Congress communications director Matt Raymond, is to document "important tweets" as well as gather information about the way we live through the sheer masses of tweets on the site." (Hope, 2010)

Ever hear of the Way Back Machine and the Internet Archive?

It's this "little" project of over 150 billion, yeah, billion pages (and counting) of archived web pages. Want to see what My Space looked like in 2006? You can! You can even see what some people's profiles looked like in 2006, and some people, who thought that they "deleted" their MySpace content in 2006 may be shocked to know that their images, comments, etc, still exists years later because it was archived in 2006. In practical terms, this means that content deleted since 2006 may still exist on the Internet archive -- and it will continue to exist for future generations to review. Go check this out for yourself at www.archive.org.

You Are Historic

Archiving initiatives like the Internet Archive, the Library of Congress preserving "tweets" and more are established to create reference points for future generations to be able to learn, understand and see the evolution of digital technology; to learn about who we (their forefathers) were — at the dawn of the Digital Renaissance — at the turn of the 21st century.

Just as many of us growing up had robust sources of historic information available to us through Encyclopedias, our future generations will need reference points, footage, illustrations and exhibits that demonstrate the evolution of the digital age, the Internet, and social networking. While there are a number of wonderful aspects about this Digital Renaissance that our future generations will be able to write about and report on, there will also be a number of "dark" reference points, because a True record of what our society is currently doing with digital technology *will* reflect a great deal of abuse!

Because we have such a lack of [global] Digital Consciousness, we have digital citizens posting embarrassing, sexual, exploitable, ignorant and hateful information to the World Wide Web without realizing that the content is being cataloged and archived for future generations to see, read and learn from. Future generations are going to look back and realize that along with the levels of creative and ingenious technological advancement was a frightening and rampant digital ignorance — a lack of Digital Consciousness.

For example, let's say you have a sexy picture that you took for your partner that you uploaded (from your computer) to your "private" social web page on the World Wide Web. It is a sexy picture that you would not want anyone else except your partner to see, so you tell them where they can view it. Now, for whatever reason, you decide you want to delete that picture from the web. Here are just a few ways that the picture you thought was deleted from the World Wide Web could be seen by the world — including your future generations — and why all of us must maintain a mindset that what we do digitally is public and permanent.

Scenario 1: Someone hears about or stumbles across the picture online and shares or saves it before you delete it. Here is a real example of this happening:

Images were saved out of a hacked Photobucket account in the following screenshot. What you will also notice is a discussion about pulling back images deleted by the website for **T**erms **O**f **S**ervice violations. The following image is taken from a message board dedicated to hacking or "breaking" PhotoBucket accounts. This is a prelude to the exploitation avenues and situations you will discover in Section 4.

Scenario 2: Someone who works at the website where you posted your sexy picture, perhaps quality control making sure your picture is not illegal or breaking the Terms Of Service (TOS), sees and saves or sends your photo to a friend before you delete it.

Scenario 3: Your "loved one" (accidentally) shares your picture with someone else. Then the recipient saves and sends your photo out to someone else.

Scenario 4: The web page with your "sexy picture" on it is archived. Even after you delete it, the picture may reside on an Internet Archive or "cached" server.

Regardless of the myriad of scenarios that are possible, once your picture is saved to a hard drive by any third party, your deletion of the content on the original site no longer matters as the content is already outside of your account. It is gone, and you will have no recourse to ever remove it from every web page, every message board, every hard drive on the planet once it is shared — becomes "viral."

> **Note:** These scenarios were Internet focused and did not even *touch* on the myriad of other scenarios where the picture could easily get out such as the computer (that was used to save and upload the sexy image) being stolen or lost or infected by malware.

Remember, if you post content (text, pictures, videos, files, etc) to the World Wide Web that you would not want the world to see and it "gets out," it is *you* who is accountable for the Consequences, not the Internet, not the website, not digital technology.

It is also important to understand that what you do in a digital world does not just affect you. This account comes from a 14 year old after a live event in Kansas. According to the attendee:

> "I am 14, and I was at a party after last school year where there was underage drinking. I was not drinking, but I do smoke cigarettes. A number of the girls that were drinking were snapping off pictures of themselves. One picture had 3 popular seventeen-year-old girls who posed behind a kitchen counter with lots of beer cans stacked on the counter. They were each drinking beer in the pic. Somebody posted the pictures to My Space and the next day, everyone at the party that appeared in the pictures was in a lot of trouble with not only their parents, but the school and police as well."

This 14 year old went on to reveal that he was in the background of a picture "having a smoke" and because somebody *else* at the party felt the need to post pictures of the party on My Space, anyone who was in the pictures (including this young man that thought they had "gotten away with a great party") wound up getting "busted."

How did the school and police obtain the pictures? A fellow classmate of the party hosts saw the pictures on MySpace and "shared" them with the authorities out of anger that she was not invited.

Hopefully the information and examples in this Section have revealed to you just a few of the many ways that your "private content" can become public and permanent. It is vital that we constantly remind ourselves that we must maintain the mindset that, "what I am about to do with my digital device is something I should be comfortable doing anywhere, at any time, in front of anyone."

Despite the digital device, if it has a memory card, that memory card can very easily find its way into the hands of another individual, and with it, goes all of your content as well. How can it find its way into the hands of somebody else? Let us review just a few *common* methods:

- Because you threw it out
- You sold it
- You lost it
- It was stolen
- It was hacked
- You lent it to someone and
  - then they lent it to someone
  - they lost it
  - they threw it away
  - it was hacked through their malware infected system

Don't Forget The "Pocket Dial"

Ever "pocket dial" anyone? Pocket Dialing is when a person's cell phone that is located in a pocket accidentally dials someone, unbeknownst to the person carrying it. The recipient of the call usually receives a very annoying, long and potentially incriminating message. As smart phones evolve to become faster, and to more easily connect to the web, it becomes that much easier to pocket dial "private" pictures, videos, files and texts to the Internet, other cell phones, email and more by accident!

Think about how fast you would send or share a "juicy" message that was accidentally "pocket dialed' to you with your friends.

Do you think that a recipient of *your* accidental pocket dial would not show your "private content" to their friends?

Now think about the Consequences. Think about the fact that in one second you can accidentally pocket dial out a "private" message or image that can never be retrieved, and could become public and permanent for the world. Think about the fact that if you never put that content on the hard drive to be "pocket dialed" to begin with, this situation is impossible!

Are you pickin' up what I am layin' down here? Are you starting to understand how easily your digital content can find its way into the hands of "another?" And many of the examples I have provided herein are obvious ways! Remember the story I told earlier about the reporter's memory card and how I came to see all of the pictures of those kids drinking? Well, if that story was not obscure enough for you, here is one more story that represents one of the millions of obscure, random and innocent ways that "private" content can become public and permanent.

> "It was supposed to be an assembly on the importance of donating blood, but some 400 students at Norwin High School in western Pennsylvania were treated to a slide show of hardcore pornography instead.
>
> The images, stored on a portable flash drive owned by an employee of Central Blood Bank, were not intended for public viewing but nevertheless appeared on the school's giant TV screen when an assistant principal clicked the wrong PowerPoint file. The unique show and tell presentation remained on the screen for no more than 30 seconds before the school employee got wise and pulled the plug." (Portnoy, 2010)

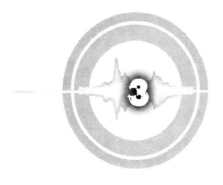

OUR DIGITAL DISCONNECT

"Intellectuals solve problems, geniuses prevent them." - Albert Einstein

The best part of a Public and Permanent mindset is that it allows us to prevent digital problems now -- and in the future. This thought system is perpetually preventative, despite digital innovation. You don't even have to be aware of trends such as sexting, cyber bullying or sextortion in order to prevent yourself from knowingly or unknowingly participating in the trend if your mindset is that your digital activity is Public and Permanent.

Think about it: Would digital citizens be taking nude pictures (that they meant to be private) of themselves with their cell phones if they truly understood how quickly those pictures could become public and permanent?

Would you?

We don't need to say or focus on an Effect such as sexting to stop sexting, we need only to prove the necessity and accuracy of a preventative "public and permanent mindset" which is the thought system that will take care of everything! Install the correct thought system, and behaviors will take care of themselves.

Prevention Offline vs. Reaction Online

Here is a question I receive quite frequently from parents:

> *"If I don't know everything my kids are doing online or with their cell phones, how can I keep them safe?"*

Well, before answering this, let's unplug for a minute and ask ourselves how we would respond to a similar dilemma, but one that does not involve technology. Let's say for instance that I was to ask those same parents the following question.

> *"If you don't know everything your kids are doing when they leave the house, how can you keep them safe?"*

Most would say that they proactively communicate life lessons and information, such as "stranger danger" so that their children could make informed decisions while they are outside of their parents' watchful eyes. Most parents realize that it is not the outside world exclusively that is inherently dangerous to their children in as much as it is the world coupled with poor or ill-informed decision making.

Now, this realization might lead us to ask ourselves, if we provide our kids with a preventative thought system like "stranger danger" to help them make preventative and informed choices offline, why are things so complicated once technology gets involved? Thankfully the answer to this question is a bit simpler — and that answer is fear.

It seems as if many individuals in our society are fearful of digital technology. Fearful of what our kids are doing with it, fearful of what criminals are doing with it, fearful of the "dangers" of the digital world. This "fear" is completely misplaced as it is not digital tools and technologies that are scary, rather the Consequences that stem from our own abuse of these tools. Only we have the power to make digital tools and technologies "seem" scary. It is our perceptions that often make digital tools and technology seem scary. But we can replace this misconception with one powerful tool: knowledge.

Our fear is based on a lack of understanding and knowledge about where responsible use of digital tools stops, and abuse starts. We are fearful of the unknown. Digital tools are nothing more than powerful tools of convenience and communication designed for our benefit. They are similar to many other (non-digital) tools that enhance our lives every day like a car or stove.

Now at this point you may be wondering how a discussion about cars and stoves is relevant to digital safety and responsibility. Truth is, the same mindset we use in protecting our children from non-digital dangers is what we all need to learn to apply to our digital lives.

When you stop and think about it, there are a lot of non-digital tools, strangers, locations and situations that present risks and dangers to us and our children *offline* every day, but we do not call our candles, cars, or neighborhood parks "scary" because we communicate accurate information to our youth about these tools and locations *before* we permit them to walk out the door.

This proactive communication of information helps parents feel better when their kids are not around because parents know they have armed their children with the necessary information so that they can make an informed decision and evaluate risk vs. reward should they come into contact with a stranger (stranger danger), fire (heat consciousness), reckless driver (defensive driving), etc.

In short, when it comes to the outside world, we provide our citizens with a collective consciousness that they can use to avoid potential dangers and pitfalls that they might encounter. So looking back at our original question in this section:

> *How can we keep our children safe if we don't know everything that they are doing with technology?*

The answer is quite simple — by upgrading their collective consciousness through the installation of a Digital Consciousness.

To help us understand the digital disconnect between how we *prevent* issues offline and *react* to issues online, let's observe the following:

- First, we will take a look at some specific offline tools and situations such as fire and strangers — and how we *proactively* communicate information or a "Consciousness" for each new generation to ensure we all have knowledge instilled in us at a young age so we can make informed decisions about fire and strangers.

- Then we will apply a "Consciousness Removal" to compare how our society is ineffectively reacting to or dealing with digital tools and technologies.

- Finally, we will discuss this comparison to illustrate the major disconnect between how we proactively communicate offline safety information and reactively communicate digital safety information, and why this "disconnect" is leading to the digital issues we are seeing, reading and hearing about every day.

So let's get start by observing how we proactively communicate information about the responsible use of fire or heat.

Heat Consciousness

Heat Consciousness can be defined as, "Playing with fire can burn you and your surroundings."

The reason why you don't put your hand in the fire is not because of fear, it's because you know that you'll get burned. You don't need fear to avoid unnecessary danger – just a minimum of intelligence and common sense. (Tolle, 1999)

I am now going to tap into your intelligence and common sense, to ask you three simple questions.

- Should we teach candle safety, stove safety, BBQ safety, hot water safety and fire-place safety separately — or — should we simply communicate to society one simple and uniform guideline that "playing with fire can burn" — a Heat Consciousness — which can then be applied to any and all (heat harnessing) tools?

  If your response to this first question is to communicate one simple and uniform guideline that "playing with fire can burn," then ask yourself:

  Why we are teaching, cell phone safety, Internet safety, computer safety, etc as opposed to communicating one simple and uniform guideline that applies to all digital tools — that "digital activity is public and permanent?"

- Should we wait for children to run into a burning building because it looks pretty (like a giant fire place) to tell them that fire can burn — or — should we inform them ahead of time about the dangers of abusing fire so they understand what can happen to them if they run towards that burning building, or anything else on fire?

  If your response to this question was to inform them ahead of time about the dangers of abusing fire, then you must ask yourself:

  Why are we waiting for there to be enough victims of negative situations such as sexting or sextortion before we give these trends national attention in the media and react, as opposed to communicating one simple and uniform guideline that "digital activity is public and permanent?"

- Should we provide a child with matches, and only *after* he burns the house down, tell him about the dangers of abusing fire? Should we follow that up by charging that kid with arson for burning the house down since he was playing with matches, even though he had never been given a Heat Consciousness?

If your response to these questions were "no" and "no" respectively, then you must ask yourself:

Why is it NOT OK to hand a child matches without a Heat Consciousness, but it IS OK to hand a child a digital device without a Digital Consciousness? Why is it OK to wait for (inevitable) negative trends to become main stream news — only after there are thousands of victims — and then arrest children for their abuse of digital technology when they were never provided the information to know what the consequences of their actions could be?

Heat makes for an excellent analogy to digital technology as many of us use and rely on heat and heat harnessing tools on a daily basis — the same way many of us [increasingly] use and rely on technology and digital tools every day.

We use and rely on fire or heat in some capacity every single day despite the fact that we all know how powerful and dangerous heat can be. We do not control fire; we attempt to harness it to enhance our lives through tools such as the candle, the stove, the grill, fire place, etc. If you ever stop to really look at fire, you may discover just how beautiful and mysterious it can be. What may really be surprising however is to think about how much damage this beautiful element could create if abused or in the hands of the wrong individual.

Ironically, despite the number of personal and national fire based tragedies society has faced through time, we are not terrified of heat when it is used responsibly, even though we know that an accident could cause a great deal of harm to ourselves and to those around us. We are comfortable using or being around heat harnessing tools because we *proactively* understand the difference between responsible use and abuse of these tools, and we have a respect for the overall power of fire.

This respect and knowledge of heat responsibility is communicated to us at a young age to ensure we grow up in the world *proactively* understanding how to remain safe around tools and situations that involve fire, despite the sometimes catastrophic results that abuse can cause. For generations we have created and mass distributed countless [heat harnessing] tools without mass fear because we have concurrently armed ourselves with a very important and preventative thought system called Heat Consciousness.

Stranger (Danger) Consciousness

Stranger (Danger) Consciousness: can be defined as, "Do not interact with a stranger."

"A stranger is a person whom you have never met. You may have seen the person before but don't know anything about him or her. Strangers don't look like monsters, aliens, or the bad guys you see on TV. They look like ordinary people." – McGruff the Crime Dog.®

- Should we wait until our children are recovered from an abduction to tell them we don't take car rides from strangers?
- Should we leave our kids alone in a school or room full of complete strangers of any age or mental health?

We don't send our kids off to the park or the mall without ever communicating "stranger danger" or instilling in them a "Stranger Consciousness" because we know that the tragic result could be that we never see them again. Let us once again refer to the question at the start of this section and modify it to inquire about going to the park instead of accessing the Internet (a global park).

> *"If I don't know everything my kids are doing (or who they are talking to) when they go to the local park, how can I keep them safe?"*

Doesn't this question seem like a "no brainer?" It is because we provide them with proactive information. We provide them with stranger danger or a "Stranger Consciousness."

We cannot be with our loved ones (kids and adults) every second of every day, thus we cannot be a physical shield between our loved ones and a predator — no matter how much we wish we could. This is why we do everything we can to communicate to our loved ones ahead of time that they should not interact with strangers. By communicating this information, we send our loved ones out into the world armed with the ability to make an informed decision, armed with the ability to evaluate risk vs. reward, armed with knowledge.

While parents may be concerned or nervous when their kids are at the local mall with their friends, we generally are not hysterical about these types of situations even though we know that predators and pedophiles "hang out" at parks and malls because these are areas where their potential victims frequent. We let our youth visit public places outside the home despite the knowledge that "strangers" could harm them emotionally and physically. Growing up and experiencing the world is a necessary part of life, so we must arm our youth with information to reduce their risks.

We do not teach "park stranger safety," "museum stranger safety" or "mall stranger safety" separately, right? We do not separate stranger danger at a sporting event from a rock concert. What we do is proactively communicate that [irresponsibly] talking with a stranger anywhere could amount to tragic consequences, and we then support that statement with information about what those consequences could amount to.

A Stranger Consciousness, like a Digital Consciousness is not just necessary for children, but for everyone, of any age. After all, how can parents or teachers communicate knowledge to youth if they lack information or possess perception?

Not too long ago, a friend of mine in her mid thirties was leaving the neighborhood supermarket which she lived close enough to walk to (and she did). She purchased more than she intended to and was struggling to get out of the market with a number of shopping bags. As she walked out of the store, a "sweet old lady" in her mid 70's offered to drive her home. My friend actually got into the car with the woman who locked the car doors for safety and pulled out of the parking lot. About 2 minutes into the ride, my friend realized that this was incredibly stupid and became very nervous. Although she got home safely, she realized that there were a number of ways this woman could have kidnapped her — the most likely being that the woman (or somebody in the back seat) could have had a weapon to make her sit still while they drove "away."

Our respect and knowledge of stranger danger is communicated to us at a young age to ensure we grow up in the world proactively understanding how to avoid an unsafe individual or situation. And even if we find ourselves in one as was the case in the previous story, at least we recognize it and proactively try to limit the potential danger. For generations citizens have been permitted to leave their home and visit public places without mass "fear" despite the knowledge that people do get harmed and abducted by others, because we have armed ourselves with a very important and preventative thought system called Stranger [danger] Consciousness.

You can find more examples and insight into my "Consciousness" methodology applied to Sex and Cars in the section titled, "More Consciousness Methodology" in the Workbook at the end of this Guide.

Consciousness Removal

So far in this section we have examined how we protect our families from fire by teaching them Heat Consciousness and from strangers by teaching them Stranger (Danger) Consciousness. With each of these strategies being communicated and used on a daily basis to keep our families safe, this naturally leads us to ask these questions:

- Why on earth are we mass distributing rapidly evolving digital tools and technologies *without* applying the same *preventative* methodology (a Digital Consciousness)?

- Why are we waiting for situations such as sexting, sextortion or cyber bullying to present themselves in order to start "dealing" with these issues? And more importantly, why are we only focusing attention on these specific issues which does *not* prepare anyone for what's coming next?

It is with these questions in mind that we begin to understand the real concern that should be associated with digital technology. In fact, the only thing scary about the mass distribution of rapidly evolving digital tools and technologies is the lack of Digital Consciousness that is accompanying the distribution. In other words, we're handing out digital tools without including the instructions for responsible use.

We must be more proactive and focus on the real problem of an underdeveloped digital consciousness, as opposed to reactive; waiting for enough individuals to find themselves at the epicenter of very serious situations before we shed light on the situations via media and then do our best to catch up. We saw this with "sexting" and "cyber bullying" and we will see this reactive pattern occur again with "sextortion." The following examples will help illustrate the significance of this severe social blunder.

In each example we will employ a reaction-based methodology to fire and strangers to help illustrate the point that it is as insane to react to digital issues as it would be to react to fire or stranger based issues.

A World Without Heat Consciousness

Picture this: Imagine a world whereby nobody was taught Heat Consciousness. What would it look like outside your window or on your local news channel if we mass distributed heat based tools like matches, lighters, candles, natural gas based stoves and grills without concurrently communicating a uniform "golden rule" that "playing with fire can burn."

Quite likely, we would observe a world that was literally on fire. Over time we may learn how to stop causing specific negative Effects like burning our hands with matches, but without a universal understanding that when abused, fire leads to tragedy, we would continue spinning our wheels dealing with continuous Effects and subsequent Consequences of this problem, instead of focusing our attention on the lack of knowledge leading to poor decision making — the Cause. Let me clarify this point through the following example:

1. Heat Consciousness: A group of individuals (young and old) are provided a heat harnessing tool called "matches" but never told that playing with fire will burn.

    Digital Consciousness: A group of individuals (young and old) are provided a digital tool called a "digital camera phone" but never told that their actions are public and permanent.

2. Heat Consciousness: These individuals burned themselves, their houses, trees, etc, with their matches.

    Digital Consciousness: These individuals took nude photos and videos of themselves with their digital camera phones.

3. Heat Consciousness: One individual burned himself so badly that national media picked up the story, labeled the Effect as "Match Burning" and sensationalized the trend.

   Digital Consciousness: One individual had their nude picture sent around their school, which prompted the national media to pick up the story, label the Effect as "Sexting" and sensationalized the trend.

4. Heat Consciousness: The media attention sparked a social movement to create surveys, safety tips, information and even congressional laws but ONLY about stopping people from burning themselves with "Matches" or from "Match Burning."

   Digital Consciousness: The media attention sparked a social movement to create surveys, safety tips, information, even congressional laws but ONLY about "Sexting."

5. Heat Consciousness: We talked to citizens ONLY about burning themselves with matches or "Match Burning." Example: Here is what you need to know about "burning yourself with matches."

   We failed to mention that "playing with fire or with any lit heat harnessing tool can harm you and your surroundings" — there was no concurrent communication of a Heat Consciousness.

6. Digital Consciousness: We talked to citizens about sexting ONLY. Example: Here is what you need to know about "sexting."

   We failed to mention that, "digital actions, with any digital tool, can become public and permanent" — there was no concurrent communication of a Digital Consciousness.

So now what happens when these individuals are given access to a stove, lighter or grill since all we reactively taught them about was matches?

Clearly, reaction here would fail. How much devastation would we permit until we communicate that playing with fire will burn, no matter what tool or situation? How long would we wait to communicate a preventative Heat Consciousness?

Here is a real scary thought. Taking this example even further: Fire is not evolving, so even if we eventually figured out how not to burn ourselves and the world through reactionary means, without ever communicating a proactive Heat Consciousness, we would *eventually* have a laundry list (obtained the hard way) of the "do's" and "don'ts" of fire use. It would not have to be updated all that often because again: Fire is not evolving. For example:

- Don't play with matches
- Don't touch a hot stove
- Don't touch hot water
- Don't play with a lighter
- Don't throw water on a grease fire
- Always put out your (campground) forest fire
- And on, and on, and on

Now take a look at what is going on in a digital world. Look at the news, or in your community at the devastation. The digital world is (figuratively) burning the same as an offline world would burn without a Heat Consciousness. But the digital world is not burning because of digital technology, its burning because of a lack of Digital Consciousness.

Unfortunately, unlike our example with fire, digital tools and technologies *are* evolving every second of everyday. Therefore, if we continue to react to digital issues by focusing all of our attention on specific trends, all we succeed in doing is perpetuating a vicious cycle of reaction, and we fail to put out the (digital) flames. As we work to resolve one issue such as sexting, newer issues such as sextortion will surface, and we will begin to feel overwhelmed, trying to tackle two issues through reaction.

Think about it like this: Waiting for issues such as sexting, cyber bullying, or sextortion to arise, and then *reacting* to them as individual and separate Effects, is like:

- Waiting for large groups of people to burn themselves with matches, and then talking to them only about match safety,

- Waiting for large groups of people to burn themselves on stoves, and then talking to them only about stove safety,

- Waiting for large groups of people to burn themselves on lighters, and then talking to them only about lighter safety,

- And so on and so forth.

Obviously the solution to safety with heat harnessing tools is to be proactive in teaching a Heat Consciousness and the same holds true for the digital environment. The unfortunate reality is that reaction in a digital world will always fail, and until we begin to effectively communicate and use a thought system that digital activity is public and permanent, society is going to continue to get burned.

A World Without Stranger (Danger) Consciousness

Now imagine a world without stranger danger. A world without proactive Stranger Consciousness, where we would wait for someone to be "taken" to try and explain to them the folly of their judgment to "go with" a stranger. Let's face it: We would be terrified to let our loved ones walk out of the front door. We would be terrified to let them go anywhere or do anything such as play at the local park, because we would not know if they would be coming home safely that night.

Now imagine after two years of incidents where people had "gone missing," the media picked up on this "trend" and labeled it "Abduction."

We started hearing, "little Suzie down the street was kidnapped at the local park" and "Bobby from two towns over was taken from the local mall." Perhaps we tried to keep our kids away from that park or the mall because "bad things" happened there. So we limited our loved ones experiences because we were filled with fear about what happened to others and what might happen to them. We had no idea how to keep our loved ones safe except to keep them under lock and key at home because we had never heard of "stranger danger."

> **Note:** There are a lot of parents who try and shield their kids from using technology due to this fear-based methodology. Parents are keeping technology out of the hands of their kids (under lock and key), but unfortunately, in doing so, they are shielding their kids from all of the benefits technology has to offer, and they are impeding their children's social and professional progress as they are living and growing in a digital world.

Then, after a while, law enforcement alerted us to the fact that people like Suzie and Bobby were taken because they got into the car of a stranger.

Our Digital Disconnect

We told our loved ones: Don't get in the car with strangers. And this is the ONLY lesson we taught them, because we reacted to what we are heard and saw in the media and from the police. So "Car Abduction" becomes an Effect, and we put our youth through "Car Abduction Safety Class." Now, because we had focused on and taken care of the Effect, "Car Abduction," we had (a false sense of) comfort sending our loved ones back out to the park and to the mall because we (thought) we knew how Abduction happened, and we told our kids, "Don't get into the car of a stranger" but we never communicated a Stranger Consciousness.

> *This would be like sending a kid (or adult) to an Effect-based class like "Cyber Bullying," but never talking to them about how to prevent all types of current and future digital issues with a Digital Consciousness.*

A couple weeks later, more news comes out from the police indicating that people were being abducted because they told strangers their names and addresses. So we created an Effect called "Personal Information Abduction" and we created a "Personal Information Abduction Safety Class." We then had parents and youth sit through this "Personal Information Abduction Safety Class" before we again felt comfortable enough to send our loved ones back out to the park and to the mall. Because we had focused on and taken care of the Effect titled, "Personal Information Abduction" we had (a false sense of) comfort sending our loved ones back out to the park and to the mall as we told them, "Don't get into the car of a stranger" *and* "don't give personal information to a stranger," but we never told them that they should never talk to a stranger, *anywhere* or at *any time.*

> *This would be like sending a kid (or adult) to an Effect-based class about "Sexting" after they already learned about "Cyber Bullying" but still never talking to them about how to prevent all types of current and future digital issues with a mindset that digital activity is public and permanent.*

A month passed. More news came out: Kids were being abducted because they took drugged candy from strangers. So what did we do? We created a "Candy Abduction Safety Class" and had our families sit through another program before we again felt comfortable to send our loved ones back out to the park and to the mall. Now we're telling them, "don't take candy from a stranger," "don't give personal information to a stranger" *and* "don't get into the car of a stranger" but again, we fail to use this as an opportunity to communicate the golden rule of stranger danger – don't talk to *any* stranger.

> *This would be like sending a kid (or adult) to an Effect based class like "safe social networking" after they already learned about "Cyber Bullying" and "Sexting" but we still never talk to them about how to prevent all types of current and future digital issues. We never communicate the 21st Century Golden Rule – digital activity is public and permanent.*

Pretty insane methodology here, no?

It seems pretty insane to wait for new information to come out about something terrible that is happening (in this example "Abduction"), over react to it by keeping our loved ones away from all public places at all times, then as information "comes in" we react to each specific situation, as opposed to using some common sense and instilling *one* uniform social norm like stranger danger which says, "do not interact with strangers anywhere at any time!"

Well this is exactly what we are doing to our digital generation. It is exactly the kind of insanity that is taking place in our society, right here, right now, in this Digital Renaissance. Rather than install a broad and preventative message into the minds of our now digital generation, we seem to be waiting for a new trend (a new way of Abduction under this example) to occur. Should we continue to race to get our digital citizens in a room, and provide them with reaction based information, after victims like Suzie, Bobby and countless others have to learn it the tragic way?

- How many of us have reviewed Cyber Bullying surveys, watched news reports, took technology away or stopped using it based on these news reports, or sat through (or had our kids sit through) Cyber Bullying classes?

  How many people in society and in Government are focused on "Cyber Bullying?"

  How does this prevent the sextortion problem?

- How many of us have reviewed Sexting surveys, watched news reports, took technology away or stopped using it based on these news reports, or sat through (or had our kids sit through) Sexting classes?

How many people in society and in Government are focused on "Sexting?"

How does this prevent people from irresponsibly over-sharing information like posting future status updates on sites like Twitter or Facebook?

We cannot undo our digital mistake once it goes viral, no matter how many parents or police we talk to or actions we take. So we can't wait for a problem or trend to surface, and then react to the information presented. To help prevent (blind) digital mistakes, we need nothing more than a mindset to help us carefully and thoughtfully think before we act with technology — we need a mindset that our digital world is not private, and that our (digital) mistakes cannot be "erased."

Parental Controls Have Holes

It was not too long ago that parents were primarily using parental controls in an effort to keep their kids from visiting pornographic websites. Suddenly, these tools have evolved to help parents keep their kids from becoming the *creators* and *providers* of adult content.

Concerned parents all over the U.S. often ask me about parental controls. One mom in California asked me the following question:

"What about using parental controls to stop the madness?"

Well first of all, parental controls typically only apply to kids, and what is far too often overlooked are the number of adults that find themselves in embarrassing or exploitable situations based on a lack of digital consciousness; but I digress.

While parental controls are great tools to see where kids are going online, who they are talking to and what they are posting, even a real-time alert that a child just posted a naked or illegal picture of themselves online will not *prevent* the picture from going viral. By the time a parent can take action based on the real-time alert, the picture will already be online. It is "out" and because your parental controls must *react*, in this scenario, they will have failed. Parental controls, safety tips, and assessments are wonderful and beneficial tools and should be used, but they are typically reactionary tools designed to catch abuse. They are designed to compliment, *not replace*, a Digital Consciousness.

Parents Just Don't Understand

Parents Just Don't Understand is a famous song released in 1988 by DJ Jazzy Jeff & The Fresh Prince (a.k.a the multi-talented Will Smith). It rocks — and it's true! Parents will never be able to keep up with, or on top of everything "new" that kids will do and discover with rapidly evolving technology. This is not a new trend. How many baby boomers were masters of Nintendo? How many parents (despite the generation) will know the cool new school fashions until their kids inform them?

Older generations will always be behind the "trends" set by younger generations, and it is unreasonable to expect parents today (just as it would have been 20 or even 50 years ago) to know about every single (digital) trend that kids are involved in before their kids get "involved!"

Unfortunately however, a child of the 21st century can almost instantly make a (digital) mistake that could alter their entire legacy which is a situation that children and parents of previous generations did not have to worry about. It is this fact that creates fear and frustration for many 21st century parents. Learning about a (new) digital issue or trend that "all the kids are doing" because it happened to your child can be terrifying — so why wait? The good news is, you don't have to!

While parents should make every effort to know what their kids are doing in a digital and non-digital world, parents no longer *have* to know about every new digital trend before they can:

- Talk to their kids in an effort to prevent an issue,

- Help their kids be responsible digital citizens, and

- Inform their kids about the appropriate and responsible use of digital tools and technologies!

Parents no longer have to cross their fingers and hope that their kids do not find themselves at the epicenter of some new digital issue, becoming nothing more than a statistic of another problem! What parents must do to ensure their child is armed with information to make an informed decision — even though they may not always make a wise decision — is to communicate a preventative mindset to help their kids understand how to avoid any new negative trend or issue — and that mindset is that digital activity is public and permanent.

The Rickety Bridge of Technology

A live national television interview with a teenager about a cyber bullying incident illustrates an ironic "disconnect" between generations stemming from our heavy utilization and reliance on digital technology. While technology has bridged borders and generations online, it has ironically created a gigantic chasm between generations offline.

Let me explain:

In June 2010, on a live television broadcast, a 13-year-old female said the "c" word or "c*nt" twice during the same appearance as she described text messages leading up to a tragic event. (Katz, 2010)

What was surprising to many, however, was not only the fact that she would say that word twice on live national television, but that she said it without blushing, without embarrassment, like it was NBD (No Big Deal). One viewer's online reaction — similar to many — was:

"I can't even get that word out of MY mouth. I am shocked when kids say things like that. I wouldn't chastise her for it or anything, but yikes."

Digital tools and technologies such as the World Wide Web have bridged our borders and our generations in so many positive ways. For example, a 50 year old in New York and a 15 year old in California can share thoughts and ideas on education, current events or recreation such as a debate about the outcome of a New York Jets win over the Oakland Raiders via a football-related message board. Technology makes it possible for anyone, anywhere to share and communicate thoughts, opinions and ideas without the *need* to know or share anything "personal" or "private" about each other.

However, what "older" generations must understand is that our youth (and the generations to follow) are living, working and playing in a digital world, and spend a great deal of time "online" with 30, 40, 50+ year olds who are talking and acting like 30, 40 and 50 year olds. Our youth has been desensitized to "foul language" and other "adult situations" because they are spending an enormous amount of their time on a platform created and used by *all* of us; and not all of us filter what we say and do on It.

Before the implementation of the World Wide Web, there was limited exposure to vulgarity and nudity if you were a minor. Before the Internet, it was difficult for minors to gain access to sexually explicit pictures in an adult magazine or see and hear adult-related themes and language in movies, but that does not mean they did not want to. Today, however, extremely graphic adult related content is just one click away, and what's worse, many minors are becoming the providers of this adult related content through their own irresponsibility as I will explain in greater detail in Section 4.

We must remember that we have 10, 11, and 12 year olds sharing the same platform as 30, 40 and 50 year olds; so when older generations talk like "adults" online (e.g. how much a team "sucks" or I hate my "sh*tty" job), our youth will always be a part of this conversation. For every pro, there is a con, and while we can now share creative, informative and entertaining thoughts, ideas and opinions about anything, with anyone, anywhere — the cost of this amazing communication medium is the fact that the line between being a "kid" and an "adult" has been severely blurred.

NARCISSISTIC VOYEURISM AMPLIFIES EXPOSURE - IT'S ALL FUN AND GAMES UNTIL SOMEONE USES AN EYE

"We who have touched war have a duty to bring the truth about war to those who have not had a direct experience of it. We are the light at the tip of the candle. It is very hot, but it has the power of shining and illuminating." – Thich Nhat Hahn

Most of us use digital technology. And we all know that our tech tools provide us with a "window to the world." But sometimes we forget that a window works both ways. Habitually using digital technology maliciously and irresponsibly can put a digital target on our backs, exponentially increasing our chances of becoming a victim of unwanted attention and being exploited.

Being on the "front lines" in schools and communities across the United States, I see and hear some of the devastating Consequences of poor digital judgment that affect real people of all ages. These experiences cause me a lot of sorrow and frustration when I see how many situations could have been prevented. For that reason, I remain motivated and committed to communicating the necessity for everyone to obtain a Digital Consciousness. Because it is crystal clear to me that there are too many citizens in our digital world that do not fully grasp, understand or comprehend the tragedies and challenges that they can cause for *themselves* in just a *moment* of poor judgment. The knowledge and information in this section are just a few of the tragic consequences that stem from poor digital choices. I hope this is enough to persuade you to adopt a Digital Consciousness.

I want to reiterate that my goal in this Section (and Guide) is *not* to scare or deter anyone from using digital tools and technologies. Let's face it: Using technology isn't optional. We *must* use it in order to thrive in our rapidly evolving digital world. However, for the same reason many of us were required to watch videos of car crashes in driver education class, I feel I need to provide real examples of how dangerous the Consequences of poor judgment can be — and trust me, there are consequences of poor digital judgment far worse than what I am willing or able to share here.

I feel it is important that you at least obtain a glimpse into some of the *real* Consequences that can stem from poor judgment, so that you can make a knowledgeable and informed decision *before* using digital devices. Some of what follows may be scary, but remember, it is not digital technology that is scary, rather the situations stemming from abuse of technology that can be frightening. Remember: It's not just digital tools – ignorant or blind use of anything – fire, cars and sex – can often lead to tragedy."

Narcissism Invites Voyeurism

Think about the gossip and privacy issues celebrities must be prepared to deal with as a result of our society's voyeuristic cravings. When we start calling attention to ourselves on a global public platform in an effort to garner attention, we must also be prepared to handle the bad and the good feedback — without the fame or fortune. Once we put the information "out" — once we turn on our very own digital "PR Machine" — we cannot turn it off!

In an offline world, we put alarms on our homes in an effort to keep ourselves and our most valuable possessions safe and secure. We keep our most intimate secrets and skeletons safe, secure and "in the closet" of our minds. Let's be honest: Not too many sane people walk around school, into work or through the community and announce all of their most embarrassing, private or "dark" thoughts and actions. However, it seems as if a digital device in the hands of a sane individual somehow "possesses" them to tell perfect strangers that they are not home, to send a "sexy picture" across a globally public platform, or to verbally assault or attack someone else in front of the world. It is bizarre!

It seems as if the mass distribution of digital tools and technologies has increased our desire to be special, unique, original and infamous. We have developed an even deeper adoration and desire for individuality in our (digital) culture. However, this seeming spike in narcissism has concurrently enhanced our society's voyeuristic tendencies (as if we are all now on a reality TV show called the "World Wide Webbers"). But many of us are getting "more than we bargained for" when the information we (sometimes irresponsibly) share to obtain "attention" is watched or noticed by people who are "less than altruistic."

Our use of and reliance on digital tools and technologies will continue to benefit our personal and professional lives, offering us powerful tools of communication to express our creativity and ingenuity. It is vital to comprehend that this is *also* the case for criminals — and it is a golden age for the "digital underground" right now. Global levels of poor digital judgment are astronomical, and criminals can strategically capitalize on this poor judgment in a myriad of ways – and they are!

The Crystal Ball Into Your Future

Do you lock your doors at night?

The same person that locks their doors and puts an alarm on their home will announce to billions of people on sites such as Twitter, Facebook or LinkedIn that they are "currently away on a business trip" or "leaving on vacation tomorrow". What sense does this make? Why would someone lock their doors and power up an alarm for their home if they are going to "undo" all of that effort by giving a billion people a crystal ball into their future? To tell a billion people, "yeah, my house may be locked, but I won't be in it!" See any insanity here?

A friend of a business acquaintance of mine was bragging on Twitter that he was going to "unplug" and go camping in the Ozarks with no technology — just his dog, tent and grill for four days. When the guy returned to his apartment, he found it completely empty.

How? Why?

Perhaps it is because he told his friends, family, community *and* criminals through a global public platform called the World Wide Web that he would be away from his apartment for four days.

You cannot hold a giant carrot in front of a rabbit and be surprised if it eats it. Telling a world of criminals you will be away is never a good idea. If you wouldn't announce in the local paper you were going away for a week, then why would you announce it through a global (digital) publication? If you would not feel comfortable leaving your front door open when you leave your home, then you sure as hell should not feel comfortable telling the global village when you are going to be away!

Here is an example of criminals "cleaning up" due to the irresponsibility of narcissistic digital citizens who feel the need to over-share information. Understand that geo-location sites that are here and evolving like FourSquare will not help to reduce this type of digital irresponsibility, but you can help yourself if your mindset is that your actions are public and permanent:

> Mario Rojas, Leonardo Barroso and Victor Rodriguez burglarized more than 18 homes in the Nashua area of New Hampshire simply by checking status updates on Facebook and then pillaging the houses of victims who announced on the social network that they were not home, according to New Hampshire's WMUR Channel 9 News. (BILTON, 2010)

Sometimes people will ask me:

> *"So what about when I tell co-workers I am leaving for vacation, or I set an out-of-office assistant that sends out an auto reply and tells people, even "spammers," that I am out of the office?"*

Here is my response to such a question:

> *"Understand that there is a huge difference between setting an "out-of-office message" for a business email account and posting a future status update on an unsecure social website such as "Twitter" or "LinkedIn". Just because you are out of the office does not mean you are not home (in fact in many cases it means you may be home) and the entire world is not emailing you at work to receive the auto reply."*

Beware the C.E.L

It is important to remember that we are all now part of one global community, global village, global park. Use whatever terminology you want to remind yourself that we now share the same digital world with everyone else (good and bad). The greater insight we give the world into our lives, the more vulnerability we inherit from criminals that also share our digital world.

Do you know how to beware the C.E.L.? The acronym C.E.L stands for **C**yber **E**xploiter of **L**ife and is defined by The Institute for Responsible Online and Cell-Phone Communication as, "any individual or organization that gains, profits or benefits personally or professionally from the exploitation of citizens through digital tools and technologies or cyber space." Basically, a C.E.L exploits poor judgment through digital or cyber activity. There are a variety of reasons that a C.E.L would exploit us if we give them a reason to. The most common reason is for money, although others exploit for revenge, and some do it just for fun. In this Section, I will offer you just a few examples of how a C.E.L exploits our neighbors, why they do it, how you can avoid it, and how poor digital judgment and exploitation affects all of us through the "Ripple Effect."

WARNING: It is very important that you understand that at NO TIME should you EVER attempt ANY of the criminal activity described herein or you may find yourself in severe legal jeopardy.

Sexting Is Stupid

Would you share sexually explicit pictures and videos of yourself with the world?

It is astounding how many individuals and organizations actually *promote* the act of sexting for adults as "fun" or "flirtatious". It is terrifying to read articles with statements like "start sexting your spouse and tell me what comes of it."

Think adult sexting is fun and flirty? Here are a few points to ponder:

- What would you do if you lost your phone and your sexting texts, images or videos ended up on the World Wide Web?

- What would you say if your friends or family members saw and shared the texts or images?

- How would you feel if your "private" photos became adult content for an illegal adult website?

- How would you react if you were blackmailed or exploited because of this content?

And finally, how can you expect your children to be responsible with technology if you fail to provide a good example for them to follow. Truth is, we don't live in the old do-as-I-say-not-as-I-do world anymore.

If we don't protect our own digital reputations, how can we possibly expect our children to develop a Digital Consciousness – an understanding that their actions are public and permanent?

I have some questions for those individuals and organizations promoting "sexting."

- What would your advice be to the individual that loses their phone with their "fun sexting" texts, images or videos on it when their friend, family member or community member finds it, sees it, and shares it?

- What would you tell them when they find their "fun" has become adult content for an illegal adult website?

- What would you tell them if they are blackmailed because of this content, or found themselves in the middle of an exploitation situation?

Here are examples of what can – and does – happen to people who have engaged in sexting – regardless of their ages.

Let's start with the most basic consequence blackmail. What would you do if you received an email that had a real (supposed to be "private") naked picture of you attached with an ultimatum that said:

> *"You will send money to the following address and you will reply to this email with more nude pictures of yourself within 6 hours. If you do not comply, the attached naked picture of you will go up onto an adult website, and it will be sent to all of your friends and family."*

Many citizens say, "I would call the police!" But what will local, state or federal police be able to do if this email comes from an individual outside of your country?

Take a look at this real-life situation:

> A northern Iowa man who threatened to publicize sexually explicit photos of his former girlfriend taken when she was a minor pleaded guilty Wednesday to child pornography and extortion charges.

> Roegner admitted that, beginning on May 30, he sent a series of messages on MySpace to a former girlfriend, threatening to post the explicit photos online unless she agreed to meet with him.
>
> One of the messages had two pictures attached that said, "...u wouldn't want anyone to see these." A later message said, "...if I don't hear back from u by next Wednesday I will post them." (Schulte, 2010)

There are a variety of ways and reasons to be blackmailed by somebody, but being responsible and having a mindset that your actions in a digital world are public and permanent will drastically reduce the odds of anything happening to you. Why? Because if you don't put questionable content "out there" then criminals won't have anything to find that could be used to blackmail you. Makes sense right?

To make sure you understand how real this threat is, here is another example of just how scary the Consequences of poor digital judgment can be:

This is a real story coming out of Ottawa, Canada. What may bother you is that this is not a rare activity on the "dark" side of the web.

> Kanata teen Ryan McCann first hooked girls as young as 14 with promises of thousands of dollars to perform via web cam. Then he tricked, threatened and blackmailed them into performing more degrading "shows" for clients of his company, [omitted]. The acts included penetrating themselves with hair brushes, simulating oral sex on flashlights until they gagged and writing "dirty slut" on their breasts or "fat ass" on their buttocks. (Gillis, 2010)

What you have to realize is that the capture and conviction of the C.E.L in the previous example does not take the content of these girls off of the hard drives of his clients — or off of the web. The girls' content will be there forever. It will be part of their legacy — it is public and permanent.

Do not have the perception that this only happens to kids. In fact, it is a legally safer "play" to exploit adults for money because there are no child-related legal violations.

If the victims described in the previous two blackmail examples had a Digital Consciousness — a mindset that their digital activity was public and permanent – perhaps they would not be standing in front of their digital cameras and web cameras for "quick cash" or for "sexy fun." Perhaps these individuals never become victims of their own blind insanity because they would have possessed a thought system to prevent it!

The fact is, just a few minutes of independent research on the topic of what is now being called Sextortion (research does *not* mean participate in it) will reveal some very disturbing information about the "dark" behavior taking place on the digital black market.

However, and I cannot be clear enough, the common theme across almost all stories and situations is that the chain of events leading up to the actual blackmail and extortion starts with the victim's lack of Digital Consciousness. As you review the examples provided herein, ponder the chances of these situations ever happening if the victims had a preventative mindset that their actions would be public and permanent.

C.E.L's Selling You - Why Do They Do It?

Sexual exploitation in our (digital) world has eclipsed the status of "digital epidemic." For some reason, many people think it is primarily kids and teens who are rapidly becoming victims of their own irresponsibility.

Many groups and organizations are so concerned with minors seeing pornographic content online that many do not realize minors — and adults — are quickly becoming the premier *providers* of pornographic or sexually explicit content for the world.

Call it sexting, chexting, sexcasting, whatever you want, but understand this: While it may seem fun and flirty to take and send sexual pictures of yourself or a loved one, the consequences that stem from digitally documenting yourself or others in "sexy" or "sexually explicit" situations can make you an instant (global) pornographer.

There are tens of thousands of individuals in this world who are "ignorant pornographers." In other words, they have no idea that their poor digital judgment to create a sexy picture or video of themselves is being exploited by C.E.Ls for profit. There is no better way to start an adult website than to do so with $0 in start up costs. I will expand on this exploitation avenue in a moment, but first let me reiterate how important it is that you DO NOT TRY THESE EXPLOITATION AVENUES, METHODS OR IDEAS or it is likely you will wind up in jail, or worse — especially if you live in the United States where operating an adult website requires compliance with United States Code: Title 18, 2257.

As I mentioned, an extremely popular trend in the digital black market is a C.E.L's propensity to use other people's "private" content to create lucrative networks of adult content. Everyday millions of image and video files are taken from "private" web pages, cell phones, digital memory cards and other digital devices. This stolen sexy content is used to build and operate illegal adult blogs, websites and networks.

> **Note:** There are legal adult websites established to "look like" their content is amateur or "stolen." I am *not* referring to these, or any other legitimate adult websites that legally compensate their adult performers, supply an 18 USC SECTION 2257 compliance statement (United States Code), adhere to federal laws and run legitimate and legal adult video chat services. Further, while website owners in the United States are held to stringent legal standards for maintaining janitorial records of the individuals portrayed on an adult website (18 USC SECTION 2257 compliance), this is not the law for all countries. Understand that a porn website with your sexy pictures on it out of Russia is still accessible by citizens in the U.S. and around the world regardless of whether it adheres to U.S. Law.

Think about this for a moment. Tens of thousands of people exhibit sexually explicit behavior in front of webcams, cell phones, digital cameras and a myriad of other digital devices everyday without understanding the potential Consequences — without a Digital Consciousness. So why would any C.E.L that owns an adult website pay for sexually explicit content (pay professional talent) to populate their websites when they can simply take and use content from irresponsible digital users and make a profit?

How They Do It - Is Your Neighbor Working With A C.E.L?

It does not make sense from a time or financial resource standpoint for a C.E.L to try and hack billions of web pages or digital devices on a chance that they *might* find something sexually explicit to exploit.

Therefore C.E.L.s set up what I call "hubs" online in the form of message board posts, classified ads, press and more to draw in people who hand deliver victims. Let me explain: Similar to abuse and crime in the real world, online abuse and exploitation often starts with friends, family members and acquaintances. Many digital citizens do not realize if they are hacked or exploited that the individual setting them up to be hacked or exploited is frequently someone they know. In other words, if you are going to be hacked or exploited, it will most likely not be the result of some international man of mystery who randomly selected your account or device to hack out of billions. Rather, it will likely be somebody you know that will throw you to the wolves. It only takes one person in your school, workplace or community to see a post by a C.E.L. like the ones provided for in Exhibits A and B to put you at risk. However, you are only at risk if you have been irresponsible and have exploitable digital content to "find".

> **Exhibit A:** The following images in Exhibit A are censored screenshots (they are not censored online) of actual public posts made in August and September 2010. These images illustrate "the dark" hubs (in this case, a message board) set up online to entice individuals into posting pictures of their classmates, co-workers and neighbors with hopes of seeing them in a sexual or exploitable situation. These posts will become "leads" for criminals. These hubs established by C.E.L's are sometimes set up to target specific states, area codes, a workplace or even school, whereby a potential victim's friend or neighbor can send in an image with a request for "sexy content" or "the goods."

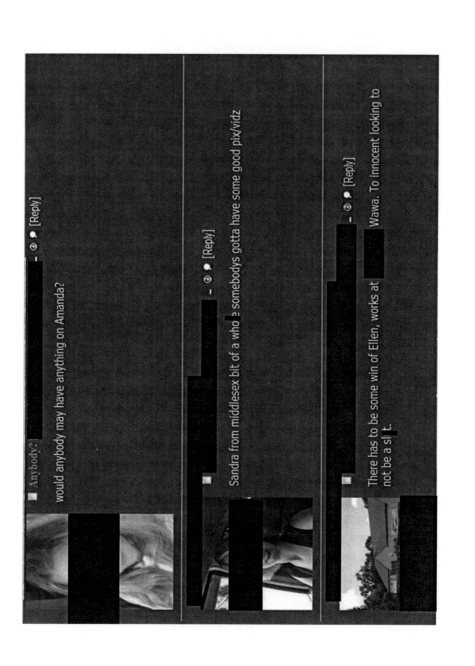

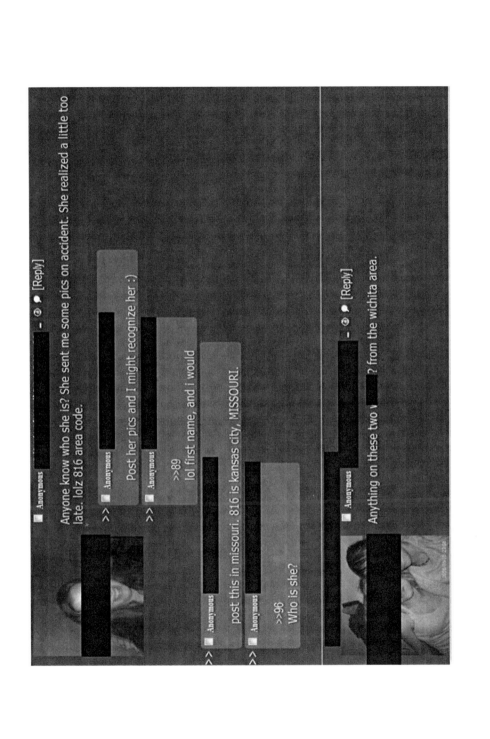

I would like to reiterate a very important point here. If you are responsible and never create exploitable digital content to "find" — even if a friend of yours or someone who sees you in Wawa does throw you to the wolves — then you cannot find yourself in an exploitable position. A Public and Permanent mindset will protect you from exploitation and blackmail even if you are hacked. How does this work? Because there will never be anything for a C.E.L to find that you would not be prepared for anyone in the world to see, and therefore, there will be nothing to hold against you; no leverage to exploit you.

> **Note:** Posting an image of a friend on a dark board to get a C.E.L to hack them for "sexy pictures" is putting that friend into a spotlight being watched by criminals. We cannot ignore the fact that sexual exploitation of an individual on a global public platform puts that individual at greater risk of a predatory attack as the public distribution of their sexually explicit content will reach a vast number of predators. Predators used to seek out victims in their local communities, but now our "local community" has evolved into a global neighborhood. Thousands of predators may now take an unhealthy (offline or online) interest in anyone they see, from any location. The (global) sexual exploitation of victims such as those seen in these Exhibits will only enhance an unhealthy obsession for thousands of predators.
>
> **Exhibit B:** The following is an image of an actual public post made on January 14, 2010. Understand that when you post content to the World Wide Web (or a digital device); there *are* people like this who have access to it:

☐ **see your friend, girl friend, ex naked** ■ 01/14/2010(Thu)02:54:05 No. 1064
[Reply & Quote] ■ ◎ ❌ ◘ [Reply]

i can pretty much garantee nudes from any girl on myspace. so if there is a friend of yours? someone you go to school with? and ex girl friend, your buddys gf, your sister? whoever you want to see naked please contact me by email ▮▮▮▮▮▮▮▮▮▮▮▮com and send me their myspace url and within a week or so you will be able to see nudes of them.

Are you "creeped out" by the fact that the word *sister* was in that post? I am!

So how can this C.E.L. accomplish what they claim they can do? Here are just a couple methods.

Someone sees this post (or one of the millions of similar ones online) and sends the C.E.L a URL of a person they go to school with, work with, saw online, previously dated, wants blackmail material for — there are thousands of reasons why someone would send the URL to the C.EL.

Scenario 1: The C.E.L visits and hacks the MySpace page and discovers nude pictures inside the account. They will save the pictures to their hard drive and walk away with content to exploit. Remember, this is an example of a "hub" where it looks as if the C.E.L is offering a public service for you to see a friend or co-worker naked, but what they are *really* doing is fishing (and possibly phishing you) for content for themselves. They make a post like this to entice users to deliver potential victims to the C.E.L. so the C.E.L. does not have to spend time and energy trying to hack millions of accounts. Make sense?

Scenario 2: The C.E.L visits and hacks the MySpace page and finds no nude pictures of the potential victim, *but* there are exploitable pictures such as underage drinking, drug use, cheating, or anything that can be used against the individual who owns the account. The C.E.L saves the exploitable content, and then blackmails the victim into sending the C.E.L nude pictures using a method similar to the one previously provided:

"You will send a nude picture of yourself and if you don't, the attached files will be sent to your friends, family, and the police."

Understand that even if the victim complies, chances are good that the C.E.L will either continue to blackmail the victim, and/or send the content out regardless. Of course, the C.E.L will also most likely use the nude pictures sent by the victim for an adult website.

Scenario 3: If someone sends the C.E.L a URL and there are no nude pictures and nothing exploitable, the C.E.L. may look for enough information to assume the identity of a spouse, girlfriend, boyfriend, etc, and try to entice the image out under false identity. There is a real example of this scenario provided a little later in this section on pages 105 and 106 whereby the C.E.L executed a "false identity" initiative through Stickam.

Of course, the scenarios in these Exhibits are nothing for you to be personally concerned about if you have a Digital Consciousness, because having a mindset that your digital actions are public and permanent means that you already understand *before* you take any responsible or irresponsible digital action (such as posting a picture of your dog on Facebook, or a video of yourself at Walt Disney World® on YouTube or a sexy video of yourself on PhotoBucket) that everyone in the global village — now and forever — including a C.E.L may see what you are about to do.

Webcams Are a C.E.Ls Best Friend

Let me elaborate on one of the most tragic trends taking place in our digital community – the exploitation of citizens via webcams.

Many popular mainstream social platforms available are very much like Facebook or MySpace except that their primary focus and form of communication is live video chat. Examples include Stickam, Chat Roulette and Tinychat to name a few.

What many digital citizens do not understand is that these webcam-centric social sites are rife with sexually explicit content. Why? Because they are influenced and penetrated by C.E.Ls. Thousands of criminals participate in, monitor, and record activity inside these sites for their own benefit.

Let me be clear when I give this warning. Participating in a sexually explicit situation in front of a webcam on a social platform (e.g. a site like Stickam, chat roulette, tiny chat, etc) — even a "quick flash" — understand that it is *very* likely that these actions will be recorded and uploaded to an (often times illegal) pornography website. This exploitation process is a common practice by C.E.Ls on many mainstream webcam-centric sites, however, I will not name all of these sites to ensure I do not garner interest, traffic or victims for C.E.Ls and pedophiles frequenting and abusing them.

Tens of thousands of individuals have no idea that shortly after they exhibited sexual behavior in front of their webcams, they were exploited. The colossal joke on the victim is that in many cases, the person they are watching and flirting with, the person enticing them to flash their private parts is often a pre-recorded video made by a C.E.L or footage of another victim. Sometimes a C.E.L performs a live sexual act in front of a webcam to entice someone else to watch or participate in sexual behavior, and the C.E.L proves they are "live" or "real" and not a recording by waving to the camera at the request of their potential victim, but what you will never see from the C.E.L is their face. Meanwhile, their victim is being recorded and exploited.

Let us use the images in Exhibit C and D to illustrate these exploitation practices.

> **Exhibit C – Using pre-recorded video loops to capture content:** This back-and-forth conversation is between multiple C.E.Ls talking about using pre-recorded video loops to capture exploitable video. Sometimes, the pre-recorded videos being "looped" are video recordings of previous victims being parlayed into more content for a C.E.L who is running the video and then recording and capturing their screen to garner adult (and blackmail) content from unsuspecting men, women, boys and girls. Keep in mind while you review this one communication string, out of tens of thousands, that millions of individuals have access to this content, and there are citizens reading and learning from it. However, this should not bother you if you have a Digital Consciousness, because you will never find yourself in an exploitable position if your mindset, while you are using your web camera, is that what you are doing will become public and permanent.

▮ 10/09/10(Fri)19:05 No. 230

I've got a good loop of this one dude that i found on ▮ It works pretty well actually. Almost every girl stops to talk. I have a good 3 mins before the dude starts getting naked. Usually what I do is pause it and tell them my cam froze. They buy it every time and I can then run with the conversation. The only negative is they sometimes only stop because they think the loops is "a normal guy" not looking to ▮

As for a female loop I've got two really good ones. What makes female loops easy to get win with, is a lot of the girls on ▮ KNOW there are a lot of vids on there. So they will stick around just to watch it, thinking its fake.

▮ 10/09/11(Sat)02:09 No. 232

Some girls are just nieve. I have at at least two times HAD to type to type to get the girl to stop staring and participate while my loop was ▮. They ask how am I typing, I said. "with toe" and they believed it. Also I usually have a male and female loop loaded into ▮ at the same time. I have started with a female loop. They tell me they are straight. I say "ok bye" hit stop on the female loop so cam goes black for couple seconds, then started the male loop and said "hi" and they have also fallen for that. (thinking that the female loop disconnected and they reconnected to a guy.

▮ 10/09/11(Sat)05:35 No. 233

I have a good loop of a girl i capped and i use that to get more guy caps. guys are easy lol just tell them not to move the camera and ask them to wave 30 sec into the cap. you can use your imagination to make them do other things too that a girl might ask to see

▮ 10/09/11(Sat)12:45 No. 234

>>232
Naive? I agree.. some are. Some are just dumb.. or at least have really bad memory. I got win from two different girls, on two different occasions, using the same loop. lolz

▮ 10/09/19(Sun)12:48 No. 266

Answer is yes loops still work! I got a collection building up. Does anyone have a loop of a girl that says hello or waves in the beginning and chats for awhile b4 getting frisky? Thanks in advance for any leads!

10/09/21(Tue)08:15 No.275

- When I started capping back in the Yahoo days before MSN had cam capabilities and before all the web ▇ was really out I met a girl on there right away who was into other girls and was very cool w/ working w/ me to get win, her and I worked together for it for the last 7 years but most of what we got was usually from MSN or YAHOO, or SKYPE, never really got into the Stickam thing because ▇ you had to go to the sites where they were usually stupid like ▇ those girls are usually the stupid ▇ ones who don't exactly care if you aren't real they just want to have fun on cam once you get them in the mood,

10/09/21(Tue)15:39 No.277

i have 4 very good loops, 3 girls, 1 guy and if i had to give an average, maybe 5% ask to wave, the rest 95% never ask.

and my loops have maybe 1 minute chat and then naked and stripping, ▇ typing in between.

the guy is just ▇ and showing ▇ for like 30 mins and soemtimes typing. i get easy win with this too because the guy looks 'extremely hot' to girl standards.

if the girl nexts when seeing these, its gonna be too much work anyway. so better for them to next, i aint gonna waste time on sweet talking sl▇ts.

many girls just start getting undressed with me. i type once in a while sexy talk which turns them on more and thats it.

dont waste time in trying to be perfect and talking 20 mins to the bi▇ch. what a waste of time.

the only reason it takes time to get a girl is because a majority of people on those kind of sites are guys that u keep nexting.

if i really tried hard for like 10 hours or something, i would get a dozen a day, so many horny sluts out there, its not even a challenge.

Exhibit D – Using live video to capture content: This screenshot represents an image extracted from a video being used on a variety of adult websites. What this still image depicts is a male (identified in the chat box as "You:" since he is hosting and recording this session) doing something sexually explicit in front of his web camera, but you can only see his private areas — never his face. The male (the C.E.L in this case) is "performing" on this site in an effort to create an opportunity for exploitation. The victim, who is now being exploited on the World Wide Web, is identified in the chat box as "Stranger:" and once she is recorded and she exposes her breasts, this video becomes content for pornographic websites and she will forever be an "ignorant pornographer."

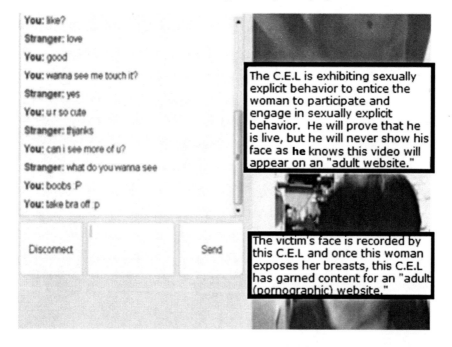

The following bullets represent two of the most frequent opportunities a C.E.L looks for in situations such as the ones presented in Exhibit C and D. These situations occur quite frequently across a number of webcam-centric sites.

- **Opportunity 1:** As he successfully did in this Exhibit D, a C.E.L will try and entice victims into doing something sexually explicit in front of their web cameras to "help the C.E.L out." Unbeknownst to the people watching and participating, the C.E.L will record the screen — this screenshot came from the video he recorded. If an individual responds to his request for "assistance" by exhibiting sexual behavior in front of their web cameras, he will use that video as content for an adult website — he has obtained free and exploitable content.

- **Opportunity 2:** A C.E.L may fail to entice individuals into to do anything of a sexual nature in front of their web camera. However, the C.E.L will successfully take a screenshot (a picture of the screen such as the one illustrated in Exhibit D) and then blackmail individuals who were watching the C.E.L do something sexually explicit. Taking screenshots of citizens' faces watching a C.E.L do something sexually explicit only takes the push of a button. C.E.Ls use the screenshots to blackmail those individuals because — let's face it — not too many people want friends, family or co-workers to see their faces on a webcam watching sexually explicit material (legal or not).

Note: The pornographic sites that provided adult content based on the practices described in this section are not legitimate adult websites that legally compensate their adult performers, supply an 18 USC SECTION 2257 compliance statement (United States Code), adhere to federal laws and run legitimate and legal adult video chat and content services such as Playboy or iFriends. In fact, I would recommend that legal adult websites dedicate resources toward the removal of illegal porn sites that exploit citizens to offer adult content as it diminishes both market share and revenue of legitimate providers.

Too many unsuspecting victims think they are "just having fun in a harmless, flirty and private" web chat. But the cold hard truth is — this collective mindset provides C.E.Ls with lucrative businesses. Take a look at the following three examples:

1) Site listings and descriptions that exploit the irresponsibility of digital citizens.

2) Software that can be used to record your computers screen.

3) Excerpts from news items about C.E.Ls and websites exploiting individuals. The individuals being exploited in these news items each stood in front of a webcam and were recorded by a C.E.L. They ignorantly provided free adult content for illegal pornography sites.

Example 1: Warning! If you do not wish to view highly graphic and sexually explicit text descriptions, do NOT try the following exercise. And if you elect to try this exercise, search at your own risk.

Step 1: Visit a major search engine such as Google or Bing.

Step 2: While every search site is different, many offer you an option of filtered or safe search results in the settings. Look for the settings link on your search engine's homepage, and make sure your "safe search" or "adult filter" is ON — yes ON — as you will be surprised what you will find even with the filters ON.

Step 3: Try performing a search for the clean and non-adult related search term "stickam girl" or "tinychat girl."

Step 4: Review the search results but do NOT click on any of them!

You will find descriptions for websites that capitalize by exploiting people who didn't realize that their actions in front of their webcams were being recorded for adult websites. Here are my top three results

- Watch nude stickam videos of girls doing wild stuff in public and private chatrooms. All for FREE.
- Over 200GB of stickam movies FREE
- [This adult website] is home to the biggest: stickam captures database site in the world.

IMPORTANT: If you decide to do your own research by searching for "stickam girl" or some other keyword or phrase, please search at your own risk. I strongly recommend that you do NOT visit ANY of the sites that you come across. Doing so not only adds to the exploitation of the victims, but it also poses both security and legal liability issues for you. To be clear, I will reiterate; if you elect to do your own independent research for more information about this malicious trend and exploitation method, it is highly recommended that you do NOT click into the actual websites in the search results and I absolutely do not recommend or condone anyone's visitation, participation or use.

Example 2: A variety of software programs allow users to record their computer screens, or more specifically, webcam chat sessions. While this software has are many positive uses, it also has malicious ones — such as recording and exploiting private chats on various webcam-centric sites. Here's an example:

- "Capture Webcams, streaming video, full screen, part of the screen and even video with sound. Use Webcam Video Capture to make people witness what you want to convey through an audio-visual medium. There are times when sharing exactly what you see on your screen is the quickest and clearest way to communicate. You can capture and anything, any window, part of the screen or full screen to AVI or WMV video formats."

Think about that: Anyone – friends, family members, frenemies and C.E.Ls – can use software that will allow them to record their computer screens. This means any time you're web chatting, there is a chance that the conversation is being recorded – whether you know it or not. Let's say you and a friend are web chatting, and that friend is recording the chat without your knowledge. The truth is, that person who recorded you may not have any malicious intent. However, the conversation was still digitally preserved – which means it could go viral in a myriad of ways. Are you OK with that? If you have a mindset that your digital activity is public and permanent, you don't have to worry about participating in recorded web chats because your public and permanent mindset will ensure that you don't say or do anything in front of a webcam that you wouldn't want the world to hear or see.

Example 3: Published in The New York Times, the news item titled, "Three Sex Crime Arrests Among Stickam.com Users So Far This Year," illustrates how real this very dangerous trend is. In part, the article stated:

- A man was indicted on nine felony counts on charges of using Stickam to trick underage girls into removing their clothes and performing sexual acts live on the Web. The C.E.L video-recorded at least one such session and later posted the video to the Web. Two other teenage Stickam users subsequently came forward to say this C.EL. tricked them as well, according to court documents. The man told the F.B.I. he collected more than 100 webcam videos of girls he met on Stickam by posing as a teenage boy. (Stone, Three Sex Crime Arrests Among Stickam.com Users So Far This Year, 2009)

While the "buzz" word for this type of activity is "sextcasting" what is most important is not focusing on the Consequences of this Effect (sextcasting). Instead, the dissemination of knowledge — a Digital Consciousness — will help prevent more victims from being exploited while national media continues to "blow the roof" off of *this* rapidly growing and dangerous trend.

What the article from *The New York Times* in Example 3 should have also pointed out is that participating in the exploitation of digital citizens will most likely land people in "legal hot water" so DO NOT TRY THIS AT HOME!

If you are angry, scared or frustrated with the individuals and groups known as C.E.Ls taking advantage of the massive amount of poor judgment in our digital world, let me give you some insight into the mindset of a C.E.L:

> *"Your ignorance is my gain! Hey man, I am just a squirrel tryin' to get a nut in this world. I go to work every day just like you, however my job is to take the content that YOU give me on a global public platform — a platform we share — and use it to my advantage. If I make money off of a nude picture of you found in your Facebook account or a nude video of you that I recorded while you were being sexy in front of your webcam, why should I feel bad? You are the Cause, I am the Effect. You took the picture, you stood in front of your webcam, you took your clothes off, and you did it on the World Wide Web, so who's fault is it really?"*

While it may be hard to believe, the examples of the consequences that accompany digital abuse in this Guide are tame compared to some of the situations that occur on the darkest and most disgusting sites in the World Wide Web. However, it is important to understand that none of the exploitation examples I have described pose a problem for you — and your loved ones — if you and your loved ones use digital technology responsibly every time you power up: If you have a Digital Consciousness!

Perhaps you had not heard of some of the situations described in this section until right now. It doesn't matter if you're aware of these issues – or any other future trend that develops through the abuse of technology – as long as your mindset is that your digital activity is public and permanent. Despite the effects stemming from poor digital judgment (such as sexting, sexcasting or anything else), or how bad the consequences (legal trouble, blackmail or exploitation) of an effect can be, if you have a preventative mindset – a public and permanent thought system – you will not put yourself in a position to be negatively affected.

> **Self Assessment Tip:** A lot of people search for their real names on the web thinking that they will find all of the web pages that their content is posted on. But why would a C.E.L that is exploiting you use your real name?
>
> In many cases, they communicate about you using a nickname, your username, email address or slight variation thereof (from the account you were exploited through). For example, if you signed up for a web chat site such as Stickam under the name "fun1", and you did something in front of your webcam that could cause you to be exploited, then a search for your real name may not reveal anything. But searching "fun1" or "funone" on search engines or C.E.L based boards may reveal some surprising results.
>
> Remember, there can only be surprising results if you lack a Digital Consciousness, if *you* do something with digital technology that you would not be OK with the world seeing.

While I will provide a couple more examples illustrating that there are some very depraved ways that people are being exploited, and why you should not try to exploit anyone unless you are willing to go to jail, I will clarify that there is really no way for me to elaborate on *all* of the forms of exploitation that currently exist as I would certainly not want to be a "hot bed of ideas" for (potential) criminals, nor do I care to expose any potential personal, professional or national security threats stemming from poor digital judgment — not to mention, tomorrow there will be a new issue, and another one after that.

The good news: A C.E.L. can only exploit you if you provide them with the means and information necessary to do so. You are in control, and your responsible use of digital tools and technologies can prevent an exploitation situation. How you protect yourself from being exploited by a C.E.L is extremely simple and effective. Maintain a mindset that your digital is activity is public and permanent. If everything you do in a digital world is something you are OK with the guy in Exhibit E seeing, then you cannot be exploited.

Exhibit E: This is a screenshot of a C.E.L who was recorded "on screen" watching and possibly recording webcam activity inside Tinychat.

As you review the following news items, think about the possibility of each situation occurring if the victims had a mindset that their digital activity was public and permanent.

- A male tax attorney was accused of allegedly blackmailing an ex-lover into sending naked photographs of herself. When she threatened to tell FBI about his demanding e-mails, he threatened to post a scandalous video montage of their sexual encounters on the Internet. One such email was allegedly sent while the 44-year-old was vacationing with his family. The e-mail contained allegedly contained the following message, "Just to give you a head's up. I've been doing a little editing on our video. Mostly some blurring of myself so that I won't be recognized. You, on the other hand, can be seen very clearly having the time of your life being f---ed by me." After an investigation, the 44-year-old was arrested and charged with extortion and harassment. (Signore, 2009)

Of course there is absolutely no excuse for the behavior of the criminal in the previous story, and in my humble opinion, he should be punished to the fullest extent of the law. With that said couldn't this situation have been prevented if the ex-lover never provided the 44-year-old with exploitable content?

Another example:

- An investigation has found that reputable Internet chartrooms and communication platforms are being used by pedophiles and sexual predators to groom children as young as 10 for sex.

  In each of the following examples, pedophiles used Skype to find their victims:

  A 50-year-old professional and father of two arranged to meet a reporter who he believed to be a girl aged 14. He turned up at a railway station near his home after arranging to take her to his home to "watch a video." The man, who said that he thought the girl's clothing would "look great on his bedroom floor," greeted a reporter who he believed to be the 14-year-old by draping his arm across her shoulders.

  A 33-year-old company supervisor and father of one attempted to get a reporter masquerading online as a 13-year-old girl to send him lewd pictures of herself and to attend a pornographic photo shoot at a friend's "mansion".

  A 32-year-old engineer took delight in ordering a "13-year-old girl" to engage in a sex act. He also told her to buy "sexy" underwear and boasted that he had just "bedded" a 16-year-old.

Once again, there is absolutely no excuse for the behavior of the criminals in these examples, and they should be punished to the fullest extent of the law. With that said, could these situations have been prevented if the victims never interacted with "strangers in the global village?"

The point is, sexual exploitation and blackmail are just examples of countless Consequences that stem from Effects; and whether those Effects are sexting, sextcasting, or cyber bullying really doesn't matter, because focusing on Effects is futile. Doing so will not prepare us for tomorrow's trends, tomorrow's exploitations, tomorrow's criminals. As technology evolves, so will the methods in which criminals use technology for their own purposes. Therefore, we cannot just sit around and wait for a C.E.L. to find new ways to exploit us. We need to eliminate their ability to do so by being responsible with our digital tools and technologies.

The Ripple Effect

The poor judgment of individuals has a vast ripple effect on communities and nations. Think about the amount of time, resources and money being spent by communities and governments to focus on Effects such as sexting and cyber bullying as opposed to a preventative philosophy or Golden Rule that prepares us for almost any potential issue, and places real accountability on all digital citizens.

Think about the financial resources required (salaries, facility management and utilities and transportation) to investigate, prosecute and jail (house) not only the most malicious cyber criminals, but individuals without a Digital Consciousness who find themselves in very serious legal or personal trouble *without* malicious intent?

Think about the time and energy law enforcement must spend trying to not only deal with egregious situations such as a predator tracking a child online, but also (unfairly and unreasonably) being expected to clean up a citizen's personal mess such as a boyfriend or girlfriend who irresponsibly sent their significant other — who quickly became an "ex" — a picture that they want the police to now "get back". Local, state and federal law enforcement have enough on their plates in the way heroically keeping us safe. Each of us could do a great service for society by independently obtaining and practicing a Digital Consciousness so law enforcement's focus can remain on the most egregious threats to society by (cyber) criminals, instead of the events and situations that stem from irresponsibility that we cause ourselves.

So let's review. There are billions of digital citizens in the global village, and the chances of you being targeted specifically by a random stranger are very low, unless you are calling a great deal of negative attention to yourself through your activity. As discussed, people who are individually selected to be "hacked" or "exploited" *directly* by another individual are typically the victim of somebody they know.

A lack of Digital Consciousness blinds us to the potential Consequences of our poor digital judgment. Does having a Digital Consciousness make you immune to all digital issues? Of course not, just as having "street smarts" will not guarantee that you will not be mugged, raped or murdered. But having a public and permanent mindset *does* reduce the chance of facing a myriad of negative and life-altering situations arising from poor digital judgment — having a Digital Consciousness prevents us from becoming the catalyst for our own misfortune.

MAKE PUBLIC AND PERMANENT WORK FOR YOU AND YOUR LEGACY

An individual without information cannot take responsibility. An individual with information cannot help but take responsibility - Jan Calrzon

A wise teacher teaches through approach, not avoidance. (Foundation for Inner Peace, 2007) We cannot hide our heads in the sand and hope that nothing bad happens when we use digital technology, and then decide to react when a situation arises. We don't seem to do this for other aspects of society such as sexual health or driving instructions, so why should this be the case for our digital use?

Failure to communicate a Digital Consciousness to digital citizens will often result in reaction to an irreversible issue. It is inevitable. It is as inevitable as handing somebody a book of matches with no information about responsible use and then being forced to deal with a burn. The following excerpt comes from an article in the Washington Post which illustrates the reality: Reacting to digital issues is failing our youth. This is a real-life situation in a middle school where the victims of exploitation were classmates of C.E.Ls — who in this case — were not international criminals, but middle school students exploiting their peers:

> Students at a Bethesda middle school bought, sold and traded inappropriate photos and videos of fellow students, according to school officials. Educators at Pyle Middle School said they were alerted to images on a student's iPod Touch. Students told school officials that the images were of girls from Pyle Middle School and Whitman High School and that they had been passed around for at least several months. The Pyle Middle School Principal made this statement, "We had no idea this was something we'd have to address. The unfortunate thing for students is that once this information is out there, it's out there. You can't get it back." (Johnson, 2010)

What keeps me up at night are statements (and I hear it all the time) like "We had no idea this was something we'd have to address." Honestly? This is a very scary, reaction-based notion, and it proves that many parents and education systems are failing our youth. Kids like the ones in this situation are certainly at fault for their actions, however:

- Did they know the potential Consequences of their behavior before they took action?

- Did they ever receive knowledge to help prevent the situation?
- Were they offered information to ensure they can be fairly held accountable for their actions?

Take a moment to form your opinion to these questions.

Now, I would like to reiterate some of the questions that I previously proposed:

- Should we provide children with matches, and only *after* they burn the house down, tell them about the dangers of abusing fire?
- Should we follow up by charging those children with arson for burning the house down since they were playing with matches, even though they had never been given a Heat Consciousness?

Now I ask you:

- Weren't these kids given a book of matches (digital tools), and only *after* they burned down the house (exploited their fellow students), they learned about the dangers of abusing fire (irresponsible use of their digital device)?

  I have to assume this is the case when I read a statement like, "We had no idea this was something we'd have to address."

- Should we follow that up by charging them with arson for burning the house down if they had never been given a Heat Consciousness (a Digital Consciousness)?

  And finally, despite the punishment these boys receive for their actions, if those pictures were ever posted online, the pictures of those girls will not come off of the World Wide Web, or hard drives of anyone who downloaded the images. Perhaps if the girls and boys had a mindset that their digital activity was public and permanent, the girls would never permit inappropriate pictures to be taken; thus, the boys never have content to get themselves into serious trouble.

Based on years of conversations with parents, teachers, school administrators, law enforcement and military personnel across the U.S., it seems as if there are many citizens, communities and institutions that do not want to make it *seem* as though they have a "digital abuse" problem. It seems that there are citizens, communities and institutions content to do nothing preventative about their "digital abuse" issues out of fear of what their community members or other communities might think. Typically, parents, communities and institutions that wait for issues to happen to react eventually wind up trying to place band-aids over hemorrhaging wounds instead of preventing the injury in the first place. But why are there communities that think like this? Many schools offer sex education to their students, but that doesn't mean that they have rampant pregnancy and STD breakouts. It simply means they are trying to *prevent* it.

If we sit back and wait for a problem to happen, to potentially ruin a life or a future, and then react, we do ourselves and our future generations a great disservice. Throwing reaction-based statistics and tips at citizens after a problem exists will not always work, and it is not fair to those individuals that had to (blindly) learn the hard way. Now is absolutely not the time as parents to subscribe to the mindset of "not my kid" because dealing with an issue after evidence is discovered that a problem exists may be too late.

Public and Permanent = An Informed Decision

I will refer you back to Section 3 and these questions:

- How many of us have sat through or had our kids sit through Cyber Bullying classes? How does this help with the sexting problem?

- How many of us have sat through or had our kids sit through Sexting classes? How does this prevent people from irresponsibly over-sharing information like posting future status updates on sites like Twitter or Facebook?

It is up to each of us to ensure that our friends, family and community have the mindset that digital activity is public and permanent. It is up to each of us to be ambassadors of this 21st century golden rule for the benefit of current society and future generations, ensuring that any and all issues that arise from poor digital judgment stems from *informed* poor judgment.

"Public and Permanent" ensures that individuals have an opportunity to evaluate risk vs. reward and can be aware of the potential Consequences to themselves and their community *before* they act.

Of course there will still be kids and adults that find themselves in hot water even if their parents, communities and institutions took a preventative approach and communicated preventative safety information. Teens are still contracting STD's even with "sexual health class" in schools, and adults are still being arrested for drunk driving, despite the fact we all know it is illegal. But landing in hot water with information to "know better" is far different than facing difficult challenges stemming from actions taken without information. Now is not the time as educators, parents or digital citizens to put our heads in the sand, or succumb to denial. By doing this we are avoiding an issue that may produce life and legacy altering situations for ourselves and our family — issues that we can actually *prevent*. Ask yourself this question:

- Who's to blame if an authority figure handed a child a gun — never gave that child information about the dangers and consequences of abusing that gun — and the child accidentally shoots a classmate?

Perhaps you have heard the old adage, "You made your bed, now you must lie in it." Well, I would prefer that the beds that we make and use through our use of digital technologies be large, fun, beds with built-in refrigerators, televisions, computers and other bells and whistles — and not cold, lumpy cots. What's more, however, is that I would really prefer if we were making our beds knowing *ahead of time* what kind of bed (a fun bed or a cot) we were making, as opposed to waiting to see what happens *after* we blindly use our tools and technologies. If an individual has information to make an informed decision, and they do something irresponsible to cause problems for themselves, then that is their fault, and they should sleep in the cold, lumpy cot as a result. But does it seem right that someone should sleep in the cot if they made a decision without the information necessary to *know* they were making a poor decision? Isn't it better to make an informed mistake than to be blindsided by something you had no idea you were doing?

An informed decision, whether or good or bad, is always better than a blind one!

21st Century Insanity

The mindset for anyone, of any age to believe they can be publically or "privately" uncensored with digital tools is best described as 21st century insanity. With the mass distribution of rapidly evolving digital tools of communication that permit us to instantly share thoughts and ideas with the world, there seems to be an underlying and unconscious craving to be outrageous and uncensored — doing things we would not "normally" do. This must be reeled in.

We have tools and a medium (the Internet) at our disposal that allow us to simply "act" without thought, discretion or evaluation. But these tools are windows to the world — and too many digital citizens are shouting things out of these digital windows that we would typically not do offline.

Think about it: Without technology, would we:

- Tell a world of strangers we're not home
- Mail a sexy picture on a whim to a (potential) loved one, or
- Threaten and harass an individual or group?

Probably not. In the offline world, most of us think first – and act responsibly as a result.

Leaving Your Digital Legacy

Prior to the digital age and society's severe lack of communication tools, only individuals of great power and stature such as George Washington, Abraham Lincoln or Napoleon Bonaparte were chronicled in our history books. We simply did not have the technical, human or communication resources to focus on "the small stuff." We could only focus on individuals and organizations that were truly making a difference in our world (positive or negative). However, today this is not the case. Today, in the 21st century, at the start of the Digital Renaissance, we are all in control of very powerful tools of communication, and we are each writing our own history. We are creating our own [digital] legacy, and what we leave behind for future generations to know about us, is entirely up to us.

Would you not want the ability to play a high definition, 3-D video of George Washington crossing the Delaware? Imagine seeing and hearing the *real* George Washington, what he *really* saw, what he *really* said and not just some re-enactment! Would you not want the ability to see this same quality video about Genghis Kahn, Socrates or Abraham Lincoln? What about your great, great, great grandparents? Do you not desire an ability to hear and see every generation of your blood line moving and talking as they were — and not what others tell you about them? The point is, *your* future generations, your great, great, great grandkids, nieces, nephews, and so on are going to be just as curious about where they come from. They are going to be just as curios to see and hear *you* in full high definition living color. So ask yourself, "When my future relatives research me using their far more powerful digital tools and technologies, what will they find out about me?" What is it you want them to see and know about you?

You *must* have the mindset that with every action you take with your digital tools, you are leaving behind your digital legacy. You are essentially creating an encyclopedia about your life that will be available on much more advanced versions of sites similar to Spokeo.com or Ancestry.com that will condense your digital activity into one public and easy to find location. When one of your (future) relatives is assigned a history report on their forefathers, what do you want them to know and write about you? Do you really want them to see what you did or posted last week, last month, 5 years ago or tomorrow?

If you passed away tragically tomorrow, what will "we" find on your digital camera card, your computer's hard drive, your web page or your cell phone? What will happen if these devices are thrown away after your funeral and a stranger or loved one views them or recovers the hard drive?

There are already family history websites such as Ancestry.com pioneering digital genealogy. Today you can go to their site to learn about your ancestors. Maybe you will find a picture, or some words, maybe a document with their signature. We cherish these facts, photos and relics because we are curious about our past, our history and our forefathers. Unless your ancestors were of historic significance, (depending on how far back you are looking) you will not find a "treasure trove" of information about them because there was a severe lack of communication tools. But this is not the case for you and your relatives. Every day that you operate a very powerful tool of communication, you also ensure your future generations will not share this "lack of information" problem. Remember, once you put something on a digital memory card or the web, it can only go "out," it cannot come back!

A Digital Awakening

Train yourself to maintain this thought system as you use and rely on your rapidly evolving digital tools and technologies.

- I am aware of the personal and global issues caused by digital ignorance and irresponsibility, and I am committed to cultivating good citizenship for myself, my family and my global community by using my digital tools with a Digital Consciousness.

- I am aware that poor digital judgment betrays my ancestors, my parents, my community and my future generations, and I will strive to eliminate the violence, fear, anger, ignorance and confusion stemming from digital abuse by understanding, practicing and communicating the mindset that my digital activity is public and permanent.

The Buddha said that our perceptions are very often false, and since error is there, suffering is there also. We must pay very close attention to this. We have to learn how to look at our perceptions without getting caught by them. In most cases, our perceptions are inaccurate, and we suffer because we are too sure of them. (Hanh, 2009) You don't have to be a Buddhist to realize the truth and wisdom here, especially when it comes to replacing the perception of digital privacy with the knowledge that there is none. How many people had to learn this lesson through suffering — the hard way?

I cannot help but wonder what positive change or shift in [digital] consciousness we would see in society if every commercial, advertisement and packaging for all digital tools provided a statement that said, "Be prepared for your actions with this product to become public & permanent." What company or organization will take the first step toward placing responsibility back onto the user by communicating knowledge and not perception?

Think about this: If you were a smoker in the 1940s, you probably had no idea that cigarettes could harm your health and the health of those around you because tobacco companies neglected to communicate information to their customers about the Consequences of using their products. Because of the lack of information communicated, these tobacco companies wound up paying a healthy sum of money to many of their victims, such as in the case of Lukacs vs. Phillip Morris:

> In June 2002, a Miami jury held three cigarette companies liable for $37.5 million in a lawsuit involving an ex-smoker who lost his tongue to tobacco-related oral cancer. (Tobacco Products Liability Project (TPLP) – a division of The Public Health Advocacy Council , 2002)

However, today we see the Surgeon General's Warning on tobacco product packaging, ads, everywhere, in an effort to provide knowledge about the negative effects of tobacco use. This information — this knowledge — is provided to place responsibility back on the user. If you want to smoke, it is your right to (if you are of legal age). However, if you are a smoker today and you fall ill because of your smoking, then *you* must take accountability, *not* the tobacco companies.

Why?

Because you, unlike our ancestors, *have* the information to make an informed decision about smoking and tobacco use.

Isn't it a shame though? Isn't it sad to think about how many people had to lose their lives and loved ones before a change was made? Before accurate knowledge about smoking was communicated to society? Do you see a pattern here? Do you see history about to repeat itself? Only this time the defendants will be various technology companies and services that create and mass distribute tools and technologies with no warnings or accurate information to put responsibility back on the user.

Perhaps if digital technology companies and services were equally concerned about communicating prevention through knowledge as they are about how fast their networks are with the 3G, 4G, tastes great G, less filling G ad campaigns, there would be less negative Effects with technology. The faster the "G" the faster you can make an irreversible mistake, and *that* is fact, *that* is knowledge — but who is telling you that?

The message that your digital actions are public and permanent is simple, clear and gets the job done. It makes users understand what they are about to do could affect them forever. It installs the correct thought system to use digital tools responsibly, and repetition of this message on every digital tool, and every ad for every digital tool would create mass awareness and shift our consciousness. It would install the right mindset ensuring we communicate knowledge — not misperception — to our digital citizens, and place responsibility and accountability back onto each individual where it belongs.

At the end of the day, our financial and human resources must be reallocated from focusing on specific issues to mass communicating and proving the effectiveness of the public and permanent mindset. If users of digital technology have a mindset that their actions are public and permanent, if they have the information to help them make an informed decision, then the accountability of their actions can fairly fall on their shoulders.

The very powerful digital tools of convenience we have at our disposal are awesome. They should be used as much as possible to benefit our lives because that is what they are for. We cannot hide from technology, and we cannot hide our youth from technology. We must embrace it because digital tools and technologies are only going to continue to evolve. They are not going to disappear, and why should they? The fact that I can read about my beloved New York Jets from anywhere at any time on my phone is most excellent. However, with great power *does* come great responsibility, and we need knowledge to know if we are being responsible or not. Poor or blind judgment in a digital world can transform powerful tools of convenience into weapons of self destruction in seconds. If you believe your actions in a digital world are public and permanent, then you have the mindset – the knowledge – to make an informed decision.

Our Digital Evolution

Our Digital Evolution is mandatory! As digital technology continues to evolve, so must our minds, as our use and reliance on this miracle will only grow. There are but two choices that each of us has before us:

1. The act of reaction, or
2. The act of prevention.

We can spend the rest of our lives trying to avoid becoming a victim of our own digital ignorance, hoping to avoid negative trends and situations, praying that we do not (blindly) become an *example* of a new issue or a statistic — *or* — we can live our digital lives understanding how to harness the power of digital technology responsibly to our benefit. This second choice allows us to know how to keep ourselves from becoming a statistic and how to leave behind a positive digital legacy.

Global change will not happen overnight. Change in how we, as a global neighborhood use and influence one another through digital technologies can only happen as expeditiously as we practice and teach Digital Consciousness. Our civilization's Digital Evolution cannot happen without a change in mindset, and periods of change are not always easy or comfortable. Change will require each of us to challenge the way we currently use our digital tools, and question whether or not we are employing them as powerful tools of convenience and communication, or weapons of self (and community) destruction. Global change starts with you, and here is some advice to get you started:

> **Self Assessment Tip:** Each and every time you power up any digital tool (camera, computer, Internet, cell phone) try and picture a family member, friend, child, enemy, criminal, whoever means the most to you in this world standing right over your shoulder, and then apply the following mindset. The more you think this way, the quicker it will become second nature to you and prevent you from crossing the line of responsible digital use, into digital abuse, where tragedy often occurs.

- If you are truly OK with the person that means the most to you in this world seeing and knowing what you are about to, and you are ok with what you are about to do becoming a part of your digital legacy, then go for it.

- If you are NOT OK with the person that means the most to you in this world seeing and knowing what you are about to, and you are NOT OK with what you are about to do becoming a part of your digital legacy — then DO NOT DO IT!

> This final bullet is the answer for anyone who wonders where the clear line of responsible digital use stops and digital abuse starts — the clear way to define digital use vs. digital abuse.

- You are NOT OK with the person that means the most to you in this world seeing and knowing what you are about to do, and you are NOT OK with what you are about to do becoming a part of your digital legacy, becoming public and permanent — BUT — you do it anyway.

This is the very simple yet effective mindset to help you know and understand how to avoid abusing ANY digital tools and technologies! If you can avoid the behavior pattern in this final bullet, then you know how to prevent any digital issue — you practice with a Digital Consciousness — your mindset is "public and permanent."

Only you have the power to enhance or harm your future through your own decision making.

It is my sincere hope that this Guide has provided you with the information to know and understand how to be digitally responsible — conscious of your digital actions. The next time you find yourself at the helm of a digital device, or in a position to influence a group of digital citizens, emerge as an ambassador of Digital Consciousness, to correct the Cause; thus proactively protecting yourself, your community, and your future.

Remember, it is not how much you know about digital technology that determines how Digitally Enlightened or Consciousness you are, rather, how you use and apply the knowledge you now have which will ultimately determine your (digital) future. So please, I implore you, understand this knowledge to be true that when you use digital technology, you must maintain a mindset that your actions are public and permanent.

I would like to thank you for taking the time to review this Guide and for caring about our global village and all its citizens. If we all shared the same passion, millions of current and future lives would only stand to benefit from the vast creativity, ingenuity and imagination of our evolving digital world.

Today we are each in control of very powerful tools of communication, and we are each writing our own history, creating our own legacy. What you leave behind for your future generations to know about you is entirely up to you. We are each very unique, very special and very talented, and we all have the ability to touch the lives of billions INSTANTLY! So make Public and Permanent work FOR you! Bless the world with a beautiful picture, poem, song or story that only you could create! You can be one of the most beautiful people on this planet — leave behind an incredible legacy — and you can do this no matter how old you are, or where you live thanks to the power of our digital tools and technologies.

So Be Amazing – Rock The World!

My name is Richard Guerry, and I am from IROC2 - Cheers!

APPENDIX: THE WORKBOOK

SELF ASSESSMENTS – GUIDANCE – INFORMATION

You can find continuously updated resources and information related to the information and exercises in this Guide and Workbook at www.publicandpermanent.com.

THE DECLARATION OF DIGITAL CITIZENSHIP

As the author of the Declaration of Digital Citizenship, I think it is important that digital citizens understand that the foundation for the creation of "The Declaration" largely stems from my opinion that we must reallocate the bulk of our time and resources away from reaction to digital issues and proactively provide the mind with the information necessary to understand that we are each independently accountable and responsible to wholly obtain and practice with a Digital Consciousness before utilizing any digital device.

I am very proud of The Declaration of Digital Citizenship and the fact that international safety organizations continue to translate this piece into their native language to ensure every member of our global village, despite their nationality, has one uniform resource to reference as guidance towards understanding how to become a responsible digital citizen in our now rapidly evolving global neighborhood.

The Declaration of Digital Citizenship

Becoming an informed and responsible citizen in our global village is a vital developmental task necessary for anyone utilizing and relying on evolving digital tools and technologies. Obtaining a uniform social guideline based on accurate knowledge, and then knowing how to apply it appropriately — achieving a digital consciousness™ — requires the integration of psychological, societal, cultural, educational, economic and spiritual elements.

Digital consciousness encompasses accurate education about the power of digital technologies and positive judgment while utilizing these technologies, as well as the ability to develop and maintain meaningful relationships; appreciate one's own self worth; interact with individuals of any age, culture and sex in respectful and appropriate ways; and express emotions in ways consistent with one's own values.

We can encourage digital consciousness in ourselves and others by:

- Obtaining and communicating *accurate* information and education about the responsible use of digital technologies;
- clearly outlining the consequences that stem from the abuse of digital technology;
- clearly illustrating that we are all now digital citizens existing in one global community or "global village;"
- offering digital citizens support and guidance to explore and affirm their own values;
- modeling healthy emotions, attitudes and behaviors when digitally interacting with others; and
- fostering and applying informed, responsible and preventative decision-making skills to all digital decision making

Society can enhance the communication and practice of 21st century digital safety, responsibility and awareness (2.1C) by providing access to comprehensive and *accurate* education and giving anyone of any demographic opportunities to receive that information.

Families, media, schools and universities, youth groups, community agencies, religious institutions, digital technology manufacturers and other businesses, and government at all levels have important roles to play to ensure all citizens in the global neighborhood have knowledge to understand and apply a uniform and necessary guideline to promote good digital citizenship and prevent social issues stemming from the abuse of digital tools (digital disease).

Society should encourage the guided and supervised use of digital technology until the end user has exhibited that they are cognitively and emotionally mature enough to be held economically, morally and legally accountable for their actions and the consequences inherited through the use of digital tools and technologies. This support should include education about:

- the public nature of digital actions;
- the permanence of actions in a digital society ;

- resisting social, media, peer and partner pressure;
- all members of society must be considered a [digital] neighbor;
- benefits of abstaining from sexual behavior through digital tools and technologies; and
- the potential economical, moral and legal liabilities of digital abuse.

Society must also recognize that many digital citizens will utilize digital tools and technologies irresponsibly for instant gratification. Therefore, all citizens should receive education and support materials to help them clearly understand and evaluate their own preparedness and digital consciousness before operating digital tools and technologies. Responsible use of digital tools and technologies should be based on a universal and preventative mindset that digital activity is public and permanent, and interaction with other digital citizens through digital means should be:

- consensual
- non-exploitative
- honest, and
- legal.

THE 21ST CENTURY FLAME

Digital tools and technologies are very powerful tools of convenience and communication, and the abuse of these powerful tools, like anything else, often leads to tragedy.

When mankind first discovered the flame, it changed our world forever. Think about how many times a day you use the benefits of heat in some capacity whether it be hot water, lighting a candle or using a stove. It does not matter if you are rich, poor, young old, American or Australian, we all use heat.

Now, through time, we have invented and employed heat harnessing tools like the candle, but until we actually light that candle, it is nothing more than a heat harnessing tool, it is not "dangerous." It is not until we light that candle that we have a real respect for that candle, because that tool is now "lit" with a flame and we know that playing with fire can burn. We know how to *prevent* a problem with that lit candle — with the flame — thanks to our Heat Consciousness.

Well we have "gone digital" so quickly, that what many of us do not realize is that mankind has rediscovered the flame — a digital flame — the 21st century flame! Unlike the traditional flame (or fire), just one moment of irresponsibility and poor or blind judgment with the 21st century flame can do more than burn you — it can annihilate your legacy.

So what is the 21st century flame?

The 21st Century flame is the memory inside of every digital device. Your digital camera, your computer, your cell phone, these are just digital tools (like heat harnessing tools) that "harness" the 21st century flame. Without a memory, your computer, camera and cell phone could not store any information. They are harmless, because they are not storing any information or data that could assist or "burn" you. A digital tool without a memory card is like a candle without a flame. However, when you "light" a digital tool with memory, you have in your hands one of two things; a "powerful tool of convenience" or a "weapon of self destruction." The choice is up to you!

In the same time you can burn your hand on a candle by fooling around (an instant); you can snap an "irresponsible" picture with a digital device like a digital camera or cell phone. The burn on your hand may go away in a week or so — the consequences are temporary; but that digital picture could be eternally public and permanent — the consequences could haunt you (and your future generations) for the rest of your life, especially if it falls into the hands of a criminal.

A GUIDE TO DECISION MAKING – SELF ASSESSMENTS

Remember, you cannot be a victim of digital technology! You can only be a victim of your own irresponsibility when using digital technology. If you harm someone while driving a car while intoxicated, you don't blame the car, you blame yourself. If you burn down the house playing with matches, you don't blame the matchbook, you blame yourself. If you contract a sexually transmitted disease from having (consensual) unsafe sex, you don't blame the disease, you blame yourself. If you do something irresponsible with digital technology and alter your life, you cannot blame the camera, you cannot blame the computer, you cannot blame the web site, you cannot blame the (relationship) ex, you cannot blame the hacker, you cannot blame the virus — you can only blame yourself. You must, and will, take accountability if you neglect or abuse the awesome power of digital technology, and this Guide and workbook was designed to help you understand and "see" the line between responsible use and abuse, to help you proactively avoid finding yourself at the epicenter of a very serious situation without even realizing that you are in one or headed into one.

As you walk through each self assessment exercise, remember that the steps and criteria for you to practice are not meant to communicate that you have no privacy in the world, only in the digital world. You must understand that if you "do it" with a digital tool, you have to have the mindset that what you are about to "do" is going to be public and permanent.

Self Assessment Exercise 1

Each time you power up any digital tool (camera, computer, Internet, cell phone) picture a family member(s), friend, child, enemy, criminal, a deceased loved one, whomever means (or meant) the most to you in this world standing right over your shoulder.

- If you are truly OK with the person who means the most to you in this world seeing and knowing what you are about to, and you are OK with what you are about to do becoming a part of your digital legacy — then go for it.

- If you are NOT OK with the person that means the most to you in this world seeing and knowing what you are about to, and you are NOT OK with what you are about to do becoming a part of your digital legacy — then DO NOT DO IT!

- If you are NOT OK with the person that means the most to you in this world seeing and knowing what you are about to do, and you are NOT OK with what you are about to do becoming a part of your digital legacy —BUT — you do it anyway; then you are abusing your digital tools and technologies!

Self Assessment Exercise 2

Train yourself to maintain this thought system as you continue to use and rely on your rapidly evolving digital tools and technologies.

- I am aware of the personal and global issues caused by digital ignorance and irresponsibility, and I am committed to cultivating good citizenship for myself, my family and my global community by using my digital tools with a Digital Consciousness.

- I am aware that poor digital judgment betrays my ancestors, my parents, my community and my future generations, and I will strive to eliminate the violence, fear, anger, ignorance and confusion stemming from digital abuse by understanding, practicing and communicating the mindset that my digital activity is public and permanent.

Self Assessment Exercise 3

When you leave your home with any digital tool whether it be a digital camera, cell phone, MP3 player, anything with "memory" (I will stress cell phones and digital cameras here, even MP3 players that shoot video and take pictures based on their, usually smaller size), be willing to hand that digital device to anybody, at any time and let them look at the memory card, let them "recover" or "un-delete" the memory card right in front of you.

If you are willing to walk out of your home with ANY digital tool, and you would not mind anyone seeing anything on that device, you are using your technology responsibly. If you are NOT willing to let anybody, at any time inspect and recover your device's memory card, then you are abusing digital technology because you do not understand that you are just one second from losing it.

Self Assessment Exercise 4

Try to think in these terms when using the Internet. Forget passwords and forget privacy. When you post information to the World Wide Web about yourself or someone else, you are communicating as part of an intimate global community. You are essentially posting information on a community bulletin board in the town square. What you must consider before you post any information is that everyone in the world (with Internet access) has the ability to see and share the information you posted, and the more attention called to the information, the more attention you will receive (positive and negative).

Once your content has been seen and shared by even just one other person — out of billions — in the global village, you can never definitively remove the information from the knowledge base of the community because anyone who has seen and saved it, can at any time, put it right back up on the bulletin board, or anywhere else in the community, whenever they want without your permission or knowledge. Once you place your information on a bulletin board in the global village, that information is no longer yours, no longer private — and never will be again.

Self Assessment Exercise 5

If you are going to leave your house with a digital tool like cell phone or camera, you should also be willing to print out and carry around a paper copy of all the content on your device's memory card. If you are not willing to do this, then you are abusing digital technology.

If you lose the printed [paper] version of your device's memory card, it would take some time and effort to send the content around the world. It would have to be physically brought to a location to be digitized, then sent to a digital device and then distributed. However, if you lose your digital device with that same content it takes only a second for whoever finds it to push a button and send it around the world. So if you would not be willing to print out and travel with the content on your memory cards, why would you be willing to store and travel with digital copies of the content on your digital memory card?

Self Assessment Exercise 6

A lot of people that search for their real names on the web thinking that they will find all of the web pages that their content is posted on. But why would a C.E.L. that is exploiting you use your real name?

In many cases, they communicate about you using a nickname, your username, email address or slight variation thereof (for the account you were exploited through). For example, if you signed up for one of these web chat sites under the name "fun1", and you were being exploited, a search for your real name may not reveal anything, but searching "fun1" or "funone" on search engines or C.E.L. based boards may reveal some surprising results.

Remember, there can only be surprising results if you lack a Digital Consciousness, if *you* do something in front of that web camera that you would not be OK with the world seeing.

Self Assessment Exercise 7

What is your digital risk spike? The Digital Risk Assessment is located at www.iroc2.org and it helps to illustrate how much negative attention you are calling to yourself based on your digital behaviors.

Before you take the assessment, take a moment to learn more about the methodology and rationale for the creation of the assessment.

The History and Rationale of the Digital Risk Assessment

If a child comes home at 10:00 pm but was never given a curfew, how could they be reprimanded for coming home late, when "late" was never defined? A curfew was never communicated, so that child never had a chance to make an informed decision (positive or negative) as 10:00 approached to decide if they would "make" or "break" curfew. So how can they be held responsible?

Meanwhile, there are individuals who are facing similar unfair circumstances in our society. Phillip Alpert was labeled and forced to register as a sex offender in the United States at the age of 18 for digitally sending risqué images of his 16-year-old girlfriend to her friends and family. (Perozzi, 2010) He was made an example of as a "sexter" who must now deal with life-altering consequences stemming from serious legal charges like "distribution of child pornography" because of a legal infraction he had no idea he was committing. The tragedy here for folks like Phillip go beyond the Consequences of being a registered sex offender or even having a criminal record or facing seeming insurmountable odds towards redeeming what was once his "normal" life. The real tragedy here is that Phillip was charged with a crime after abusing his digital tools and technologies, but NEVER KNEW HE WAS DOING IT!

While Phillip must take some responsibility for his actions, what about the fact that he had no information when he was sending out the pictures to know what could happen if he did it?

Where was his opportunity to evaluate risk vs. reward — to make an informed decision?

If Phillip and his girlfriend had a mindset that their digital actions were public and permanent — a Digital Consciousness — perhaps he and his girlfriend never take and store the nude digital picture of her — eliminating the possibility of sending it out.

> **Side Note:** Think about all of the time and financial resources that went into the investigation, prosecution and probationary monitoring of this situation when, in my humble opinion, this guy is not a pedophile or sex offender; even though tax dollars were wasted to ensure we unnecessarily "labeled" him as one.

The real tragedy for Phillip, his ex girlfriend and thousands like them is that they are at the helm of very powerful digital tools of convenience (when used responsibly) that are quickly becoming weapons of self destruction because these tools are being (blindly) abused. What is terrifying is that there are millions of individuals operating digital tools and technologies every day without a Digital Consciousness, without an understanding of how and why they are crossing the "line of responsible use." They have no idea they are straying off of what I call the "line of consciousness" or "The Line" by abusing, not using, digital tools and technologies.

A popular tool created to help make the line between responsible use and abuse clear is the Cumulative Digital Risk Assessment created by the Institute for Responsible Online and Cell-Phone Communication. The assessment was conceptualized based on the increased momentum of society's narcissism and voyeurism as if they were two speeding locomotives headed towards each other until they collide creating, well, what looks like this — $\wedge$ — a spike. The Assessment helps to illustrate how much negative attention you are calling to yourself based on your digital behaviors. It consists of a series of questions that helps to cast a light on the poor judgment you may be (blindly) employing with digital tools and technologies so you can stop immediately.

The questions are very simple. The higher your score when you are finished, the more negative attention you are calling to yourself and your actions — the further you are from the line of consciousness. The more negative attention you call, the more temptation there is for "someone" to look in on you through your digital device, your "window to the world." Remember, your "window" works two ways, and all you have to do is give someone a reason to look in, and they will. However, if you stay close to the line of consciousness through responsible use, your odds of becoming a victim of a C.E.L are very low as you are one in a billion digital users.

While the Risk Assessment was conceptualized from society's increase in narcissism and voyeurism, its actual creation and execution stems from an idea far more simple. Imagine you and I are standing outside of a stadium after a sporting event, just minding our own business. There are 50,000 people standing around us, and one of them is a thief. If nobody is doing anything to call attention to themselves, then it is likely that somebody who gets pick pocketed would have been selected at random by the criminal. Now imagine the same situation, however, just prior to the thief pick pocketing somebody, I stand up on a table in that sea of 50,000 people and I hold up a sign with my full name, social security number, address, credit card number, bank card and pin and a sexy picture.

Whereas before I was just one person in a sea of 50,000 people who *might* get robbed, I have just increased my chances of facing an issue (it is not guaranteed) because like an idiot I stood up and shared all kinds of personal information with complete strangers. In fact, with that kind of information, perhaps some people in the crowd who were not thieves before will be tempted to become one considering the info I just handed to them. By standing up and sharing certain information with 50,000 people, I increased my risk of exploitation.

The Risk Assessment applies the same theory. The higher your score, the more information you are sharing with the global [digital] village and everyone that lives in it. The higher your score, the higher you are holding a bull's-eye up over your head, and the larger the bulls-eye gets (like me standing on that table in front of 50,000 people holding up information for criminals to take advantage of). However, if you maintain a low score, then your spike is low, thus you remain close to the line of consciousness. The lower your risk spike, the less negative attention you call to yourself, the less you stand out to everyone in the digital world, and the less liability you incur.

GUIDANCE FOR STORING SENSITIVE DATA

Once information is placed on digital memory, it can only go "out." However, there are steps you can take to try and keep the data on that memory card "where it is." Here are just a few suggestions, however, it is important to understand that none of these tips are guaranteed; the only guarantee you have for [digital] information not "getting out" is to abstain from placing that information on a digital device.

Tip 1: Do not *ever* leave your home with a digital device that has a memory card in it with content you would not the world to see. While there are still many ways for the content on that card to "get out" (e.g. loss, theft, hackers, accidental disposal, etc) by not taking it out of your home, you diminish the chances of losing that device, along with the content on its memory card. Therefore you minimize — not eliminate — the chances of it finding its way into the world.

Tip 2: When you are ready to dispose of your digital device, and you want to be 100% sure that the information on the memory; the 21st Century Flame is gone or "extinguished," then physically destroy the memory card. Can you format it? Sure, there are "kill" disks and formatting techniques that will "wipe" the memory card, but it you want Absolute, 100% peace of mind that the information is "gone," destroying the memory card will get the job done. Remember, the information will still be on the memory when you destroy it, but the information will be split across hundreds of pieces.

Tip 3: Use an external memory device to store all of your "private" content and never take that external memory device out of your home. Store the external hard drive in a personal safe. When you plug the external memory source into your computer (or device) to review the content, be absolutely sure that all connections (wireless, Bluetooth, LAN, dial up, satellite, etc) to the World Wide Web are severed to reduce the chances of the information on the external hard drive being "taken" by a hacker. When you are done working with your private content, safely remove the external drive from your computer, clean the cache and history of the system, run your antispyware and antivirus programs, reboot your computer, and *then,* you can reconnect to the Internet.

OPINIONS, STORIES AND DISCUSSION TOPICS

Topic 1

True Story:

Are you aware of the tragedy that befell Bryce Dixon, who at the age of 18 was arrested on charges that included transmission of child pornography? Mr. Dixon was arrested as the result of one second of blind insanity, one moment of action without a Digital Consciousness. He was arrested for sending a photo of his 16-year-old ex-girlfriend's naked breasts to another teen because he thought she had cheated on him. In a public statement, Bryce made this comment, "I made a mistake — a very small mistake. Turns out to be a big charge." (WISN.com, 2009)

My Opinion:

The tragedy here is not so much the (in my opinion unfair) Consequences that face Bryce in as much as he is facing them based on a blind decision; an inability to have Truly evaluated risk vs. reward *before* sending the picture. If Bryce and his girlfriend had a mindset that their digital actions were public and permanent, perhaps he and his girlfriend never take and store the digital picture of her breasts — eliminating the possibility of it "getting out" — becoming public and permanent. It is important to reiterate this important point — Correction of our [digital] behaviors must happen in the mind! The mind is where we make our decisions, the mind is the "Cause" of our consequences, and the mind is where correction will work — this is the source of prevention.

Discussion Questions:

1) Do you think that it is fair that this 18-year-old individual was arrested for sending a photo of his 16-year-old ex-girlfriend's naked breasts to another teen because he thought she had cheated on him?
   a. If so, why?
   b. If no, why not and what should the Consequences be?
   c. Should his ex-girlfriend face charges as the creator of the content?
   d. If so, why?
   e. If no, why not and what should the Consequences be?

2) Do you think that individuals under the age of 18 would be taking and sending nude pictures of themselves with digital technology if they knew they could be arrested for it?
   a. If so, why?

3) Do you think that individuals of any age would take nude pictures of themselves with digital technology if their mindset was that the images would become public (to the world) and permanent (part of their legacy)?
   a. If so, why?

Topic 2

Reference:

Please refer back to Section 3 and review the sub-section titled, "A World Without Heat Consciousness."

My Opinion:

Can you make the connection between the insane thought process of distributing matches, lighters, candles, natural gas based stoves and grills without a Heat Consciousness and how we are actually mass distributing rapidly evolving digital tools without a Digital Consciousness — reacting to tragic situations stemming from nothing more than digital ignorance?

Just as a match cannot light itself, a camera cannot take a picture by itself so the problem remains with the lack of digital responsibility and not with the technology itself. While it's very true that the digital world is chaotic — and can seem quite frightening — this all stems from one simple fact; that we have mass distributed digital tools without a uniform and global "golden rule" — without communicating the necessary mindset that digital activity is public and permanent.

For a real-life example of this situation, let's take a look at social networks and the problems that we have encountered while using these digital tools. In 2006 and 2007 there were many organizations talking about MySpace safety. In 2009 and 2010 these organizations were talking about Facebook safety. But how does this prepare us for the next generation of websites, applications and social networks like Face.com, Foursquare.com or Spokeo.com and so forth, and the issues that will stem from their abuse?

Discussion Questions:

1) Are you familiar with these sites?
    a. Face.com
    b. Foursquare.com
    c. Spokeo.com

2) What issues are you aware of or foresee from an individual's abuse of these websites? List them out for review.

3) Who is responsible for each issue you wrote down? The website, the end user or a C.E.L?

4) Would an individual using these sites with a thought system that digital activity is public and permanent *prevent* the issues you have written down?
    a. If so, how?
    b. If not, why?

Topic 3

Thoughts to Review and Discuss About Cyber Bullies

A Digital Consciousness for Cyber Bullies: If you or anyone you know is about to use digital technology to spew hatred across the World Wide Web, please consider and communicate these thoughts:

- Think about this for a moment: The individual or group being harassed will have digital proof that you are not exactly a "stand up" individual. Quite frankly, the instant your victim (and the world) receive your harassing note, is the instant you give everyone power over you! Your victim may now take it upon themselves to save and send the email, picture, video or file to just about anyone they want, including an employer, a principal, a parent, to anyone who will cause you grief.

- The message (ammunition) you provide your victim is not going to go away, so anything your victim has in their possession from you, they will be able to hold over your head as leverage. They could potentially affect your reputation, scholastic career or employment as all they have to do is "show off" what you did to them. What's more, so too can a C.E.L disrupt your future through blackmail should they obtain your digital blunder and threaten to use it against you.

- Before you draft and send anything malicious using a digital tool, stop and think about what your family, friends, employers or future relatives might think when they are presented with the "cowardly hate" you are about to communicate over a digital platform because you did not have the backbone to approach your adversary offline and peacefully.

- What you write today will be [digitally] available forever. Do you want your kids and grandkids to know what you are about to write? Do you want your "hate" to be part of your digital legacy? Do you want your hate to be what shows up on a page about you that your kids or grand kids search for on sites like Spokeo.com or Ancestry.com in years to come?

- Do not assume any sort of privacy when harassing someone via digital technology. A "bully" does not warrant any privacy or protection based on the malicious actions they are employing and if a "bully" is investigated (proxy or not) they will be found, just as we would all want a terrorist to be found should they be plotting against our country.

- To your family and friends, you may be the greatest thing since sliced bread, but to a billion other people, you are going to look like a jerk. When you harass someone over a global public platform known as the World Wide Web, you do not just "bully" the victim, you bully the world, and you never know who will take exception to your remarks. You never know when your victim's friend or relative could turn out to be the next Eric Harris and Dylan Klebold (the shooters behind Columbine) or the next Charles Manson or Ted Bundy (serial killers). Hurtful remarks may just move bullies to the head of a "kill list" — and it is not that hard to find anyone through the Internet.

A Digital Consciousness for Victims of Cyber Harassment: If you or anyone you know has been a victim of (digital) harassment, please consider and communicate these thoughts:

- Remember, a word or phrase is nothing more than a group of letters, and there is not one word that has ever been able to physically harm anyone else. People cannot physically hurt you with words, only you can hurt yourself by believing it, which would be foolish!

- No matter how bad somebody may make you feel, know that you are unique and special, and you have very powerful digital tools at your disposal whereby you can show billions of people how beautiful you are, so does it really matter what some cowards say while hiding behind technology? Where you live and what you do for a living does not have to define who you are as you live in a glorious point in history whereby you have access to the entire world at your finger tips. Thanks to powerful digital tools and a global platform to share your gifts and talents you never have to feel trapped, lost or alone!

- Finally, you now have documentation that your "bully" exists as nothing more than an uninformed individual blinded by ignorance. The moment you receive any negative message, you should save, copy and print it, as you are actually empowered with information to provide law enforcement or an authority figure. Try and interpret a hate-filled message directed at you as comical. While easier said than done, feel free to laugh at your harasser's stupidity, and enjoy the fact that, despite what their two dimensional "words" say, they have just caused themselves and their reputation potential problems, not you!

Discussion Questions:

1) Do you know anyone who has been bullied through digital technology?

2) Think about a time when you have been really frustrated at someone. Maybe it was a boss, or a friend, or someone that just cut you off on the road:

    - If you had no digital technology and no Internet, how would you handle it?

    - Would you ever take time out of your day to call everyone in your town or the world to vent about what just happened?

3) What are some of the things that bullying others can stop us from obtaining / achieving (i.e. a job)? List some examples.

4) How can we most effectively communicate why it is a bad idea to "bully?"

MORE "CONSCIOUSNESS" METHODOLOGY

Sex Consciousness

Sex Consciousness can be defined as, engagement in sexual relations can result in sexually transmitted diseases and/or pregnancy.

"My father told me all about the birds and the bees, the liar - I went steady with a woodpecker till I was twenty-one." ~ Bob Hope

The only thing worse than not communicating information about safe sex would be communicating misinformation. Think about this for a second:

- Would you ever misinform someone by telling them that they could get pregnant from holding hands?

- Should we wait for someone to contract a sexually transmitted disease before we instill knowledge about the health risks associated with sex?

- Should we wait until a woman's first prenatal exam to inform her about pregnancy and how it happens?

- Should we communicate to society that only a blue condom will prevent disease or pregnancy?

The fact is, without sex, *nobody* would be around to do anything! Sex is a natural and necessary part of humanity, and like anything else, sex can occur responsibly or irresponsibly producing both positive and/or negative, and often life-altering results. For generations, millions of individuals have been faced with "scary" or life altering situations after a sexual experience including (unwanted or unplanned) pregnancy, physical and emotional issues, and sexually transmitted disease. When we stop to think about it, in just one instant of poor (sexual) judgment, your entire life can be altered forever.

Despite the sometimes startling and terrifying consequences of poor sexual decision making, people are still having sex responsibly *and* irresponsibly every day. In fact, sexual relations are a daily ritual across the globe despite the fact that we all know how powerful and devastating the consequences can be. Ironically, even with the number of personal tragedies and health-related issues we may face because of sexual relations, we are not terrified of sex, because we understand how to contract and pass an STD. We know how to prevent pregnancy, and we have proactively received knowledge about safe and responsible sex so that we can make informed decisions. We have "proactive knowledge."

We do not teach herpes safety, hepatitis safety and chlamydia safety separately. We do not separate AIDS from gonorrhea in a sex education class. What we do is *proactively* communicate that the consequences of irresponsible or unsafe sex could amount to an STD *such as* herpes, AIDS, etc. We communicate to our youth that irresponsible sex can lead to negative consequences, and we then support that statement with information about what those Consequences could include.

This respect and knowledge of sexual responsibility is communicated to us at a young age to ensure we grow up in the world *proactively* understanding how to remain safe in sexual situations. For generations our society has participated in sexual relationships without mass "fear" of sex because we have armed ourselves with a very important and preventative thought system called Sexual Consciousness.

A World Without Sexual Consciousness

Imagine an 18 year old on prom night who plans to have sexual relations with her long time boyfriend, but nobody ever communicated to the couple any accurate knowledge about the potential consequences of unsafe sex; nobody ever gave them a Sexual Consciousness. Not having the information necessary to make an informed decision, the couple has unprotected sex, and the girl winds up pregnant, and with HIV because her boyfriend had been unfaithful quite regularly away at college, and did not know he had HIV.

As disturbing as the Consequences are in this story, the real tragedy here is that neither of the individuals involved had the information to make an informed decision. In this example, society failed these two individuals who lacked knowledge. They fell victim only to their own ignorance. Perhaps *with* information, they would not have unprotected sex, perhaps *with* information, her boyfriend would never become HIV positive. W*ith* information, should the outcome of this story remain the same, at least they had the knowledge to enable them to make an informed choice, albeit a number of poor ones.

Waiting for an issue such as sexting to become prevalent in our society, and then *reacting* to it, but only focusing on sexting is like waiting for large groups of individuals to contract AIDS and then reactively instructing them *only* on how not to get AIDS; never informing them that there are many outcomes of (unsafe) sexual relations like a myriad of STDs, pregnancy and emotional and physical change — never giving them a Sexual Consciousness.

Driver Consciousness

Driver Consciousness can be defined as learn and obey local, state and federal laws and guidelines while operating your vehicle.

The best car safety device is a rear-view mirror with a cop in it. - Dudley Moore

Because each of us when behind the wheel of an automobile has the power to create tragedy and destruction, because each of us behind the wheel of an automobile are essentially at the helm of a potentially lethal weapon, we have very strict rules and regulations that we must learn, practice and adhere to if we desire the (legal) ability to operate an automobile.

- Do we wait for a driver to cause a serious accident or harm someone before we communicate safe driving techniques, laws and lessons?

For the same reason we are to blame, not the car (barring no mechanical failure) if we hit someone while driving, we cannot blame a cell phone or the Internet if we operate or "drive" powerful digital tools irresponsibly. It takes just one second of poor judgment to do irreparable harm to ourselves or someone else if we abuse the privilege of operating a motor vehicle — which is why we need a license to legally operate a vehicle. We mandate training and testing to ensure drivers can illustrate that they clearly comprehend and drive according to laws and guidelines *before* they obtain a license; thus, in the event of an accident or violation, drivers will never be the victim of their own ignorance.

Does this mean that the communication of information will guarantee every driver will always make a good decision? Not at all, hence why we are all aware of violations such as speeding tickets, reckless driving, and the like. But at least the violation is handed down to a driver who knew the penalty for their actions *before* they broke the law. At least they were able to evaluate risk vs. reward *prior* to operating the vehicle. At least they had the benefit of Driver Consciousness.

Many of us use and rely on vehicles (in some capacity, whether we are driving or not) every single day despite the fact that we all know how powerful and dangerous they can be in an accident. We do not control what others are doing in a car, or the elements around us. However, knowing that every time we get into a car, it may be the last time we do anything, does not stop us from driving or getting into a vehicle. Despite the number of personal tragedies society has faced through time because of car accidents and collisions, we are not terrified of automobiles when they are used responsibly to get us from point A to point B despite the fact that an accident could do us and our surroundings a great deal of harm. We are comfortable using or being around automobiles because we understand the difference between responsible use and abuse of these "tools" and we have a respect for their power.

This respect and knowledge of responsibility is communicated to us at a young age to ensure we live in a world proactively understanding how to remain safe around vehicles (either as a passenger or pedestrian); thus the reason many of us, once legally licensed to do so, are permitted to operate vehicles in populated public areas by government, law enforcement and society, despite the sometimes catastrophic results abuse of a vehicle can lead to.

If you learn how to drive an automobile that has nothing more than four wheels, gas and brake pedals, and a steering wheel; if you truly understand how to drive this automobile safely, then it should not matter how many "bells and whistles" you are surrounded with to enhance the environment of the automobile, because the process for driving the automobile safely;

the information necessary to drive that automobile responsibly, despite its size, amenities or color, does not change. We are all aware that there are many ways to harm ourselves and others while operating a vehicle, and yet, millions of people co-exist with millions of automobiles all over the world without mass "fear" because we have armed ourselves with a very important and preventative thought system called Driver Consciousness.

A World Without Driver Consciousness

This example just seems too easy. It would not be very difficult to imagine what the world outside our window would look like if we handed the "keys to the car" to just anyone that wanted them, of any age or mental state. Clearly the world would be a very scary and dangerous place to live if just anyone could operate a vehicle without obtaining a license.

Now, I am absolutely NOT saying that anyone that wants a digital tool should be required to obtain a physical "drivers" license to operate a cell phone or access the Internet, *however*, I do question why such powerful tools are mass distributed to just anyone that wants one, of any age, maturity level or mental (health) state, *without* informing them that they must maintain a mindset that their actions are public and permanent.

If individuals were given a digital consciousness at the time they receive their digital tools, then they would understand the line between use and abuse, and therefore could (justly) be held accountable for their abuse. Like a driver who is speeding by a posted speed limit sign and gets a ticket, an informed digital user would have proactively received the knowledge to know use vs. abuse, to evaluate risk vs. reward, to know the Consequences of their actions. They would have been proactively handed a Digital Consciousness — a metaphorical license to drive digital tools.

3 FREQUENT WAYS PRIVATE CONTENT CAN BE STOLEN THROUGH MALWARE

Scenario 1: Online Shopping

Step 1: You visit an online store and make a purchase.

Step 2: You have spyware on your machine that was placed there unbeknownst to you by cyber criminals a prior to this shopping experience.

Step 3: The spyware allows the criminals to see and capture every keystroke you make including your name, credit card number, passwords and other "private" content and information.

Step 4: Your "private data" is sold on the digital black market where it is used by criminals who will profit from your information by opening credit cards, re-selling your information, and other methods, that will assist in destroying your credit, and potentially, your reputation and legacy.

Scenario 2: Email

Step 1: You get an email from a friend, bank, credit card, social site, store and you click a link inside of the email.

Step 2: The link directs you to a phishing site — a fake website that looks real — that appears to be the site you anticipated reaching. But, maybe the URL in the site uses a zero instead of a letter "O" and you miss this.

Step 3: The credit card, banking, personal information, private content, etc you enter into this (phishing) site is actually going right into the hands of the criminal who will profit from your information potentially destroying your credit, your reputation and legacy.

Scenario 3: File Sharing

Step 1: You download a file from a peer to peer network.

Step 2: Packed with the file you downloaded was a string of malicious code or malware that will turn your computer into a "zombie."

Step 3: Your computer will be used to send illicit, and sometimes illegal content on behalf of the criminals, and you will have no idea your computer is responsible for sending this content across the World Wide Web.

END NOTES

Works Cited

Antlfinger, C. (2009, February 5). *Teen accused of sex assaults in Facebook scam*. Retrieved from MSNBC.com: http://www.foxnews.com/story/0,2933,488428,00.html

Arab Times. (2010, June 17). *Thousands paid in blackmail as many fall prey to 'games' on Net*. Retrieved from Arab Times: http://www.arabtimesonline.com/NewsDetails/tabid/96/smid/414/ArticleID/155512/t/Thousands-paid-in-blackmail-as-many-fall-prey-to-%E2%80%98games%E2%80%99-on-Net/Default.aspx

BILTON, N. (2010, September 12). *Burglars Said to Have Picked Houses Based on Facebook Updates*. Retrieved from http://bits.blogs.nytimes.com: http://bits.blogs.nytimes.com/2010/09/12/burglars-picked-houses-based-on-facebook-updates/

Blue, V. (2009, January 29). *Kids Charged for Child Porn / Violet Blue: When Teens Make Their Own Porn, Who's Being Exploited?* Retrieved from SFGate.com: http://articles.sfgate.com/2009-01-29/living/17331420_1_child-pornography-boys-face-charges-nude-photographs

Buchanan, M. (2010, August 8). *Face to Facebook Showdown For School Superintendent* . Retrieved from MSNBC: http://www.msnbc.msn.com/id/38588219/

Carlson, N. (2010, May 13). *Well, These New Zuckerberg IMs Won't Help Facebook's Privacy Problems*. Retrieved from Business Insider SAI: http://www.businessinsider.com/well-these-new-zuckerberg-ims-wont-help-facebooks-privacy-problems-2010-5

Foundation for Inner Peace. (2007). A Course In Miracles Combined Volume. In F. f. Peace, *A Course In Miracles Combined Volume* (p. 104). Mill Valley, California.

Fresco, A. (2008, September 12). *Paedophiles use internet blackmail to claim victims, says CEOP*. Retrieved from The Times: http://www.timesonline.co.uk/tol/news/uk/crime/article4735360.ece

Gillis, M. (2010, May 5). *Girls blackmailed into making porn*. Retrieved from cnews: http://cnews.canoe.ca/CNEWS/Crime/2010/05/04/13825746-qmi.html?cid=rssnewscanada

Goodin, D. (2009, October 13). *Feds: bald man posing as 17-year-old secretly taped teens*. Retrieved from The Register: http://www.theregister.co.uk/2009/10/13/predator_indictment/

Hanh, T. N. (2009). you are here. In T. N. Hanh, *you are here* (pp. 28-29). Boston, Massachusetts: Shambhala Publications, INC.

Hope, D. (2010, April 14). *Library of Congress to house Twitter archive* . Retrieved from MSNBC.com: http://www.msnbc.msn.com/id/36525336/ns/technology_and_science-tech_and_gadgets/

Italie, L. (2010, June 28). *Divorce lawyers: Facebook tops in online evidence*. Retrieved from Associated Press: http://hosted2.ap.org/APDEFAULT/APTechnology/Article_2010-06-28-Lifestyles-Facebook-Divorce/id-347ddee5e64a4a15be39d9d11bf95aac

Johnson, J. (2010, April 17). *Montgomery police are investigating how middle school sexting photos were obtained*. Retrieved from Washington Post: http://www.washingtonpost.com/wp-dyn/content/article/2010/04/16/AR2010041603657.html

Joint United Nations Programme on HIV/AIDS. (2009). *AIDS Epidemic Update 2009*. Joint United Nations Programme on HIV/AIDS (UNAIDS). Joint United Nations Programme on HIV/AIDS (UNAIDS).

Katz, E. M. (2010, June 11). *Kayla Manson on Today Show: Fla. Girl Drops "C" Bomb Defending Self in Josie Lou Ratley Assault Case*. Retrieved from CBS News, Crimesider: http://www.cbsnews.com/8301-504083_162-20007423-504083.html

KidsHealth®. (n.d.). *What Are Germs?* Retrieved June 28, 2010, from Kids Health: http://kidshealth.org/parent/general/sick/germs.html

Koleva, G. (2010, September 16). *Software maker secretly sold children's chats to marketers, NY AG says*. Retrieved from Wallet Pop: http://www.

walletpop.com/blog/2010/09/16/software-maker-secretly-sold-childrens-chats-to-marketers-ny-a/?icid=main%7Chp-laptop%7Cdl6%7Csec3_lnk1%7C171225

Levinson, A. (2010, June 30). *Big Brother is watching. And blackmailing you.* Retrieved from The Daily Caller: http://dailycaller.com/2010/06/30/big-brother-is-watching-and-blackmailing-you/

LT International Inc. (n.d.). *Got RATS in your Computer? Remote Access Trojans Explained.* Retrieved June 30, 2010, from Article Lib: http://spyware.article-lib.com/Got_RATS_in_your_Computer_Remote_Access_Trojans_Explained.html

Malcolm, A. (2008, December 5). *Obama speechwriter photographed groping Hillary Clinton likeness.* Retrieved from Los Angeles Times: http://latimesblogs.latimes.com/washington/2008/12/obama-favreau.html

Martinez, E. (2010, June 25). *Nazril Irham Sex Tape: Indonesian Pop Star Detained Over Sex Tapes.* Retrieved from CBS News, Crimesider: http://www.cbsnews.com/8301-504083_162-20008870-504083.html

McMillan, R. (2008, August 1). *Researchers show new way to hack social networking sites.* Retrieved from TechWorld: http://news.techworld.com/security/102273/researchers-show-new-way-to-hack-social-networking-sites/

Microsoft Corporation®. (n.d.). *Phishing Filter: frequently asked questions.* Retrieved July 1, 2010, from windows.microsoft.com: http://windows.microsoft.com/en-US/windows-vista/Phishing-Filter-frequently-asked-questions

Microsoft Corporation®. (n.d.). *Spyware: frequently asked questions.* Retrieved July 1, 2010, from windows.microsoft.com: http://windows.microsoft.com/en-us/windows-vista/spyware-frequently-asked-questions

Microsoft Corporation®. (n.d.). *What is a computer virus.* Retrieved July 1, 2010, from Microsoft Security: http://www.microsoft.com/security/antivirus/whatis.aspx

Musil, S. (2010, February 24). *Report: Teen gets 15 years for Facebook blackmail.* Retrieved from CNET News: http://news.cnet.com/8301-1023_3-10459536-93.html

Olmeda, R. A. (2010, April 16). *Teen charged as adult in beating of Deerfield girl.* Retrieved from The Palm Beach Post News: http://www.

palmbeachpost.com/news/crime/wayne-treacy-charged-as-an-adult-in-the-572696.html

PCWorld. (2000, April 18). *Private Lives? Not Ours!* Retrieved from PCWorld: http://www.pcworld.com/article/16331/private_lives_not_ours.html

Perozzi, V. M. (2010, April 1). *Sexting': Should Child Pornography Laws Apply?* Retrieved from ABC News / Nightline: http://abcnews.go.com/Nightline/phillip-alpert-sexting-teen-child-porn/story?id=10252790

Portnoy, H. (2010, September 14). *High school teens get an eyeful when PowerPoint presentation turns X-rated.* Retrieved from Examiner.com New York: http://www.examiner.com/manhattan-conservative-in-new-york/high-school-teens-get-an-eyeful-when-powerpoint-presentation-turns-x-rated

Schulte, G. (2010, September 9). *Iowan pleads guilty to child pornography, extortion charges.* Retrieved from DesMoinesRegister.com: http://blogs.desmoinesregister.com/dmr/index.php/2010/09/09/iowan-pleads-guilty-to-child-pornography-extortion-charges/

Signore, J. D. (2009, January 7). *Lawyer Arrested After Internet Blackmail Sex Scheme Goes Wrong.* Retrieved from gothamist: http://gothamist.com/2009/01/07/when_will_people_learn_that_e-mail.php

Stone, B. (2007, July 11). *Just How Icky Is Stickam?* Retrieved from New York Times: http://bits.blogs.nytimes.com/2007/07/11/just-how-icky-is-stickam/

Stone, B. (2009, October 15). *Three Sex Crime Arrests Among Stickam.com Users So Far This Year.* Retrieved from New York Times: http://bits.blogs.nytimes.com/2009/10/15/stickamcom-spawns-three-predator-arrests-so-far-this-year/

Symantec Corporation. (n.d.). *Lifecycle of a cybercrime.* Retrieved June 30, 2010, from Every Click Matters: http://everyclickmatters.com/cybercrime/crime-map.html

Tate, R. (2010, January 11). *Why You Shouldn't Trust Facebook with Your Data: An Employee's Revelations.* Retrieved from Gawker: http://gawker.com/5445592/why-you-shouldnt-trust-facebook-with-your-data-an-employees-revelations

The Huffington Post. (2008, November 22). *Nude Pics In Phone Lost At McDonald's End Up Online.* Retrieved from The Huffington Post:

http://www.huffingtonpost.com/2008/11/23/nude-pics-in-phone-lost-a_n_145872.html

Tobacco Products Liability Project (TPLP) – a division of The Public Health Advocacy Council . (2002, June 11). *Lukacs v. Philip Morris Verdict Backgrounder and Commentary*. Retrieved from tobacco.neu.edu: http://www.tobacco.neu.edu/litigation/cases/Backgrounders/lukacs.htm

Tolle, E. (1999). The Power of Now: A Guide to Spiritual Enlightenment. In E. Tolle, *The Power of Now: A Guide to Spiritual Enlightenment* (p. 43). Navato: New World Library.

United Press International. (2010, April 15). *4 Calif. boys cited for alleged 'sexting'*. Retrieved from UPI.com: http://www.upi.com/Top_News/US/2010/04/15/4-Calif-boys-cited-for-alleged-sexting/UPI-44541271371977/

United States Code. (n.d.). *U.S. Code § 2257. Record keeping requirements*. Retrieved June 30, 2010, from Cornell University Law School: http://www.law.cornell.edu/uscode/718/usc_sec_18_00002257----000-.html

Walder, N. G. (2010, September 24). *Judge Grants Discovery of Postings on Social Media*. Retrieved from LAW.com: http://www.law.com/jsp/article.jsp?id=1202472483935&rss=newswire

Wikipedia®. (n.d.). *Tobacco politics*. Retrieved June 16, 2010, from Wikipedia®: http://en.wikipedia.org/wiki/Tobacco_politics

WISN.com. (2009, July 28). *Debate Rages Over Sexting Penalties*. Retrieved from WISN.com: http://www.wisn.com/news/20206785/detail.html